Supporting Student Mental Health

Supporting Student Mental Health is a guide to the basics of identifying and supporting students with mental health challenges. It's no secret that your responsibilities as a teacher go beyond academic achievement. You cover key socioemotional competencies in your classrooms, too. This book is full of accessible and appropriate strategies for responding to students' mental health needs, such as relationship-building, behavioral observation, questioning techniques, community resources, and more. The authors' public health, prevention science, and restorative practice perspectives will leave you ready to run a classroom that meets the needs of the whole child while ensuring your own well-being on the job.

Michael Hass is Professor of Scholarly Practice in the Attallah College of Educational Studies at Chapman University, USA. He is a licensed School Psychologist, Educational Psychologist, and Clinical Counselor.

Amy Ardell is Instructional Assistant Professor in the Attallah College of Educational Studies at Chapman University, USA. She is a former elementary school teacher.

Also Available from Routledge
Eye on Education
(www.routledge.com/eyeoneducation)

The Brain-Based Classroom: Accessing Every Child's Potential Through Educational Neuroscience
Kieran O'Mahony

Thriving as an Online K-12 Educator: Essential Practices from the Field
Edited by Jody Peerless Green

The Media-Savvy Middle School Classroom: Strategies for Teaching Against Disinformation
Susan Brooks-Young

Nurturing Students' Character: Everyday Teaching Activities for Social-Emotional Learning
Jeffrey S. Kress, Maurice J. Elias

Improving Student Behavior: The Success Diary Approach
Ami Braverman

Five Teaching and Learning Myths—Debunked: A Guide for Teachers
By Adam M. Brown, Althea Need Kaminske

The Self-Regulated Learning Guide: Teaching Students to Think in the Language of Strategies
By Timothy J. Cleary

Supporting Student Mental Health

Essentials for Teachers

Michael Hass and Amy Ardell

Routledge
Taylor & Francis Group
NEW YORK AND LONDON

Cover art by Fiona Burns and Isla Burns

First published 2022
by Routledge
605 Third Avenue, New York, NY 10158

and by Routledge
4 Park Square, Milton Park, Abingdon, Oxon, OX14 4RN

Routledge is an imprint of the Taylor & Francis Group, an informa business

© 2022 Taylor & Francis

The right of Michael Hass and Amy Ardell to be identified as authors of this work has been asserted in accordance with sections 77 and 78 of the Copyright, Designs and Patents Act 1988.

All rights reserved. No part of this book may be reprinted or reproduced or utilised in any form or by any electronic, mechanical, or other means, now known or hereafter invented, including photocopying and recording, or in any information storage or retrieval system, without permission in writing from the publishers.

Trademark notice: Product or corporate names may be trademarks or registered trademarks, and are used only for identification and explanation without intent to infringe.

Library of Congress Cataloging-in-Publication Data
A catalog record for this title has been requested

ISBN: 978-0-367-36284-3 (hbk)
ISBN: 978-0-367-40976-0 (pbk)
ISBN: 978-0-367-81026-9 (ebk)

DOI: 10.4324/9780367810269

Typeset in Palatino
by KnowledgeWorks Global Ltd.

Michael
Dedicado a Nury, la única persona con el poder de sacar a relucir lo mejor de mí

Amy
Jim, Noah, and Matthew, I love you so much.
Mom, Dad, Lassiters, Ardells, Burns, and Crawford/Madaris, family is everything. Special thanks to Fiona & Isla for the beautiful cover art.

Contents

Meet the Authors viii
Acknowledgments x

1 Introduction 1

2 Background 12

3 The First R: Relate 30

4 Recognizing Students' Mental Health Problems 53

5 Respond: Supportive Communication
   Skills for Teachers 81

6 Respond: Teachers' Role in Understanding and
   Responding to Crises and Trauma 96

7 Responding to the Threat of Suicide 125

8 Beyond Instruction: Connecting
   Students and Families to Resources 141

9 Teacher Self-Care, Self-Compassion,
   and Self-Renewal 164

   *Appendix: Questions as a Guide to the Recognition of
   Mental Health Problems* 188

Meet the Authors

Michael Hass is Professor of Scholarly Practice in the Attallah College of Educational Studies at Chapman University, where he mentors doctoral students and teaches graduate courses in assessment, counseling, and mental health intervention in schools. Dr. Hass also holds appointments as a volunteer Professor of Pediatrics at the University of California, Irvine School of Medicine, and Visiting Professor at Vietnam National University, University of Education, Hanoi, Vietnam. He has frequently traveled to Vietnam; as a Fulbright Specialist; to teach, assist with curriculum development, and conduct research.

He is currently editor-in-chief of the journal *Contemporary School Psychology,* **author** of *Interviewing for Assessment: A practical guide for School Counselors and School Psychologists*, and co-author, with Jeanne Anne Carriere, of *Writing Useful, Accessible, and Legally Defensible Psychoeducational Reports* and *Interviewing for Assessment: A Guide for School Psychologists and School Counselors.* In 2016, he was awarded the prestigious California Association of School Psychologists Sandra Goff Memorial Award for exemplary contributions to the profession of School Psychology.

His research interests include school mental health, strength-based approaches to counseling, and resilience. He received his training in School Psychology and School Counseling at California State University, Northridge, and earned his doctorate from the University of California, Irvine.

Dr. Hass has over 35 years of experience as a School Psychologist and psychotherapist and holds licenses in California as an Educational Psychologist, Marriage and Family Therapist, and Professional Clinical Counselor.

Amy Ardell is Instructional Assistant Professor in the Attallah College of Educational Studies at Chapman University. She advises teacher education candidates and teaches courses in literacy, interdisciplinary instruction, and systems thinking at both the graduate and undergraduate levels. She also facilitates professional seminars for student teachers. Prior to becoming a teacher educator, Dr. Ardell was a bilingual classroom teacher in California public schools and in the international school system, teaching grades K-5 and high school Spanish.

Dr. Ardell received her multiple subject teaching credential and master's degree at the University of California, Los Angeles. Her doctoral work in Language, Literacy, and Learning was conducted at the University of Southern California. Her research interests include social practices of literacy, especially as they relate to socioeconomic status, as well as pedagogies using systems thinking. She has published articles in *Urban Education*, *Reading Teacher*, *Journal of Literacy Research*, *Frontiers: Teacher Education*, *Journal of Language and Literacy Education*, *Literacy Research: Theory, Methods, Practice,* and *Issues in Teacher Education*. In 2021, she and her colleagues received the Outstanding Paper Award from the American Educational Research Association's Special Interest Group in Systems Thinking.

Acknowledgments

We deeply understand that nothing significant in life is accomplished without other people. This book is better because of the efforts of many. We want to express our gratitude to our colleagues Margie Curwen, Cynthia Olaya, and Jan Osborn, who read drafts and offered us insightful feedback. We would also like to thank Amy's students, Emmery Llewellyn, Tara Schrock, Kristi Kayoda, and Sarah Garcia-Gonzalez, who also generously read chapters and gave us feedback on how the book could be practical and valuable for early career teachers. Big thanks also to Sharon Bear of Bear's Research, Writing & Editing Service for her prompt and positive feedback and to Daniel Schwartz, our Editor at Routledge, for his encouragement and guidance throughout the process of writing the book.

We are forever grateful to our colleagues in Teacher Education and Counseling and School Psychology in Attallah College of Educational Studies at Chapman University. These include Meghan Cosier, Kevin Stockbridge, Margie Curwen, Cathery Yeh, Tara Barnhart, Trisha Sugita, Jennifer Kong, Zac Graycen, Anna Abdou, Randy Busse, Jeanne Anne Carriere, Amy Jane Griffiths, Kelly Kennedy, Randee Kirkemo, and Hilary Leath. Colleagues outside of our university have also sustained us, Laurie MacGillivray, Nancy Walker, Ellen Khokha, Barbara Moreno, and Elizabeth Schofield-Bickford; thank you for the good conversations. Our children's and grandchildren's teachers will never know the depth of our gratitude for their work. We are equally grateful for the incredible teaching professionals we have had the good fortune to work with and learn from across our careers. The support, encouragement, and inspiration you all have provided have made the unlikely journey from a guest lecture to a book possible.

1

Introduction

This book is the outcome of a collaboration between a teacher educator, Amy, and a school psychologist and psychotherapist, Michael. It was inspired by a guest lecture that Michael presented in Amy's class of K–12 student teachers during spring 2018. Michael's invitation to speak in a class for student teachers came about because Amy had observed that her students wanted to discuss mental health in nearly all of the situations in which there was student discussion. After a three-hour marathon of student questions ("So, my student's father has been incarcerated and [the child] is furious and sad, running out to the playground in the middle of class …"; "What do I do to help a student who is threatening self-harm?"; "How do I support a student after his family has rejected him for coming out as gay?"), it was clear to both of us that our often siloed fields of Teacher Education and School Psychology needed to collaborate more effectively to better support students with mental health problems.

Although it may be common sense that teachers need to create healthy and supportive classroom environments for their students, it also is apparent that teachers have an essential role in supporting children with social and emotional challenges. Throughout the discussion, Michael offered straightforward suggestions for engaging with students supportively, connecting students to school and community resources to resolve more complex problems, and identifying and preempting problems before they occurred. As Michael and Amy witnessed this audience of novice educators process these insights and apply them to their interactions with children, the idea of this book was born.

Why Should Schools and Teachers Be Involved with Mental Health?

Although we will go into more detail in Chapter 4, it is important to note up front that many children struggle with mental health challenges. Over the last several years, a consensus has emerged that between 12% and 22% of young people under the age of 18 have a diagnosable mental health condition that requires treatment (Adelman & Taylor, 2012); we will discuss later the implications of having a condition that is "diagnosable." It also is important to state that this number, although large, does not account for all of the children who struggle with mental health issues. There are potentially many more who have so-called "subclinical" conditions that, although not severe enough to meet the criteria for a formal diagnosis, are still serious enough to lead to significant difficulties in coping with the academic and social demands of schools.

There are many aspects to responding to these needs, and schools and teachers have important roles. Schools are a primary setting for providing mental health services for many children and have been proposed as a key part of the solution to the lack of access to services. Some research has suggested that as many as 70% of students who obtain mental health services—only a small percentage of those who need them—receive these services in schools (Burns et al., 1995; Wiley & Cory, 2013). Given this, schools are a critical component in increasing access to high-quality mental health care.

In school, teachers play a crucial role in recognizing mental health problems as they emerge and in responding supportively to these problems. For example, teachers spend more time with students than does any other person, aside from their parents or legal guardians. As a result, they are often privy to the details of students' lives. Sometimes, these details are revealed in casual conversations when a student lingers after class or before recess or through comments made as part of a written assignment. Teachers also are in a unique position to observe children. They see how children adjust and cope with academic demands and the challenging social situations that often arise at school. Because teachers interact with and observe children in various contexts, they are often the first to recognize mental health challenges and respond to students' mental health needs.

Based on these reasons, K–12 teachers are increasingly seen as having an important role in addressing the social and emotional needs of the children in their classes. This means that their responsibilities have expanded beyond academic achievement to include encouraging the development of a variety of life skills that have implications for mental health. For example, teachers frequently help students by teaching a formal social and emotional curriculum or through informal interactions that model and encourage positive communication, collaboration skills, conflict resolution, and other social and emotional competencies.

Despite teachers' active role in identifying and supporting students with mental health issues, teacher education students and in-service teachers receive little training in addressing these issues or in regard to the mental health needs of students. Strategies to respond effectively to students with mental health needs are based on (1) understanding the nature of mental health, (2) recognizing signs of mental health challenges, and (3) knowing how to have supportive conversations with students and can help teachers to feel more confident about how to respond to students. Teachers need to understand how to talk to students in various circumstances, ranging from a student's being upset about an unexpectedly poor grade to a student who is experiencing a family crisis. They must also know how to advocate for students to utilize the full range of mental health resources available in their schools and communities.

Our Perspective

Three broad perspectives influenced this book: (1) an ecological perspective on children's development, (2) a public health perspective on how we should organize mental health services in schools, and (3) a restorative and strength-based perspective on students, their parents, and the communities in which they live.

An Ecological View of Children's Development

Although community mental health providers often focus on accurate diagnoses as a precursor to treatment, we believe that it is helpful for teachers and school-based mental health providers to take an ecological perspective that goes beyond individual factors to include social and cultural influences on children's functioning. Building on Bronfenbrenner's (1977) work, an ecological perspective understands children and their development through the quality of the relationships between children and their social and physical environments. Bronfenbrenner identified four social systems that make up a child's environment: microsystem, mesosystem, exosystem, and macrosystem.

The microsystem consists of children's immediate environments, the ones with which they have direct contact, for example, home, school, and family. The mesosystem consists of the interactions among the various microsystems in a child's life, for example, home-school communication and the relationship between the family and community agencies and organizations. The exosystem includes the pervasive social and cultural structures outside microsystems that, although children may not directly interact with them, influence their lives. These systems include government agencies, local systems of transportation, and social networks outside the family. Finally, the macrosystem is the network of larger institutional, cultural, economic, or legal structures. Examples of elements of the macrosystem include laws that govern education, economic conditions that influence employment, or regulations for access to health care. Bronfenbrenner's (1977) writing predates the rise of computers, smartphones, and the World Wide Web, but there is a strong argument to make that social media now occupies a place close to, if not in, children's microsystems.

An ecological perspective gives us a broader lens through which we can view children and their lives in schools. This broader perspective helps educators to move away from the limitations of focusing only on within-the-person variables, such as symptoms or psychopathology that seldom provide enough information to help students effectively, something that psychologists are guilty of (Gutkin, 2012). Although the macrosystem and even the exosystem can seem distant and out of reach of teachers' influence, we argue that there is much to be gained by understanding that personal problems are always embedded in the context of broader social issues, even if those connections are not always obvious.

We gain a much richer perspective of children's struggles if we attempt to grasp the entirety of their difficulties and their struggles to overcome them (Mills, 1959). One only has to reflect on the impact of having a father deported after living in the United States for decades or the recent changes in the law that allowed same-sex parents to marry to understand the real and personal impact of the macrosystem on the lives of the children in our schools. Adelman and Taylor (2006) capture the impact of the macrosystem succinctly:

> The reality for many large urban schools is that well over 50% of their students manifest significant learning, behavior, and emotional problems. For a large proportion of these youngsters, the problems are rooted in the restricted opportunities and difficult living conditions associated with poverty.
> (p. 294)

Although we argue that, to respond effectively to youth's mental health challenges, it is necessary to understand and think critically about the macrosystem, it is Bronfenbrenner's (1977) microsystem and mesosystem that are most accessible to educators. Teachers can have a direct impact on students' lives by focusing on better understanding their school's resources, improving their relationships with their students, and having open and supportive communications with parents, caretakers, and other people important in their students' lives.

A Public Health Model: The Organization of Mental Health Supports

The public health model builds on an ecological approach to human development by providing a broad view of how our responses to mental health challenges should be best organized. A public health approach to mental health services shifts the focus away from providing treatment to only a limited number of individuals who have fully developed problems to promoting mental health among the entire population (Doll & Cummings, 2008; Nastasi, 2004). The public health perspective has influenced approaches such as Response to Instruction systems used to evaluate instructional effectiveness (Gischlar et al., 2019), school-wide practices such as Positive Behavioral Interventions and Supports (Horner et al., 2014; Sugai et al., 2009), and, more recently, programs focused on mental health concerns (Collins et al., 2019). These and other programs influenced by a public health perspective are often referred to as *multitiered systems of support* (MTSS; Gischlar et al., 2019).

MTSS is typically described as having three tiers or levels of support. Adelman and Taylor (2006) view each of these tiers in terms of systems. Tier 1 includes systems for promoting healthy development and prevention problems; Tier 2, systems for early intervention; and Tier 3, systems of care. For this book, we have adapted the three tiers into four: Tier 1, mental health promotion; Tier 2, mental health prevention for those at risk; Tier 3, specialized care and treatment; and Tier 4, response to crisis.

Strengths-Based Restorative Perspective

We also advocate for a strengths-based and restorative perspective that emphasizes what works in children's lives and what they need to restore themselves in terms of the people in their lives and the communities in which they live. A strengths perspective includes difficulties and limitations but acknowledges that these are not the whole story. Saleeby (2000), an articulate spokesperson for the strengths-based perspective in the field of social work, explains that "the understanding and work of people who employ a strengths perspective is driven by the search for, the definition, and employment of peoples' resources in helping them walk, however hesitatingly, in the direction of their hopes and dreams" (p. 127).

A strengths-based perspective draws upon related areas. One is positive psychology (Seligman, 2004), which has increasingly become of interest to educators (Furlong et al., 2014; Murphy, 2013). Using positive psychology as a framework, practitioners and researchers have developed interventions that enhance subjective well-being through amplifying positive emotions (Fredrickson, 2001) or qualities, such as gratitude (Emmons & Stern, 2013), hope (Pedrotti et al., 2008), or optimism (Gillham et al., 2001).

Another significant influence on the strengths-based perspective is resilience (Masten, 2014). Research on resilience grew out of research on how adversities, such as poverty or having a parent who has a severe mental illness, disrupted children's development (Luthar et al., 2000). The finding that many children seemed to do well in life despite the adversities they faced led researchers to investigate the psychosocial factors that appeared to promote positive outcomes (e.g., Garmezy, 1993; Masten & Curtis, 2000; Rutter, 2013). Researchers have found that, although children who were exposed to chronic stress often have more challenges than do those who were not exposed, the large majority still grow up to lead productive adult lives (e.g., Benard, 2004; Cicchetti et al., 1993; Werner & Smith, 2001).

Masten (2014) coined the phrase "ordinary magic" to describe how ordinary developmental processes operate to allow children to recover from adversity. Masten's model includes five broad psychosocial systems that, when functioning well, form the core of resilience. These adaptive systems include (1) attachment and close relationships; (2) intelligence, ingenuity, and problem solving; (3) self-regulation and self-direction; (4) mastery motivation and sense of personal agency; and (5) faith, hope, and belief that life has meaning. Positive psychology and resilience provide a map that allows us to identify and name strengths. Hass (2018) summarizes these strengths as:

- The quality of relationships with peers, family, and other adults.
- The presence of cognitive or academic competencies, including skills used outside the classroom.
- The presence of aspirations, goals, and plans.
- The sense that, despite adversity, there is a greater purpose to life.
- A sense of agency or confidence in the ability to affect life and meet one's goals.

In addition to identifying and understanding children's strengths, a restorative approach to working with children with mental health challenges provides a counterbalance to the stigma and exclusion that often accompanies mental health problems. Restorative practices have their roots in restorative justice (Wachtel, 2013), which emphasizes repairing the harm done by an offense rather than punishment and exclusion from a community (Zehr, 1990). In the context of MTSS discussed above, it is one of the interventions implemented after a problem has occurred (Wachtel, 2013).

In schools, restorative justice is seen as an answer to zero-tolerance policies, which are ineffective and, more importantly, contribute to the school-to-prison pipeline (Green et al., 2019). Restorative practices differ from restorative justice in that they seek to strengthen relationships to prevent problems (Guckenburg et al., 2015). This is accomplished by encouraging the free expression of emotions or affect during spontaneous interactions and participation in formal group meetings or circles and restorative conferences (Wachtel, 2013).

Plan of This Book

The goal of healthier schools via healthier children and adults is the primary theme in this text. Thus, our goal is to provide teachers and teacher education students, especially those who are undertaking their first significant roles in real classrooms, with mental health "basics" that span the needs of children and families and their needs for self-care and compassion.

This book is practical and supported by current theory and research. As noted above, one of the organizing frames is a public health model. Within this framework, we discuss the knowledge and skills needed for four kinds of teacher actions: relate, recognize, respond, and refer. Using this framework, we first address the landscape of mental health problems in the schools, the epidemiology of mental health problems, the interplay of risk and resilience, and the nature of internalizing and externalizing problems in children and adolescents. In later chapters, we focus on specific, evidence-based responses that teachers can implement when faced with a student with mental health problems. We will discuss supportive communication skills and how to connect students and their families to in-school or community resources. Finally, we will address self-care and the importance of teachers' positive mental health. We include end-of-chapter questions, practice exercises, case studies, and checklists to make the book more practical and the material accessible to educators who do not necessarily have a mental health background.

References

Adelman, H. S., & Taylor, L. (2006). Mental health in schools and public health. *Public Health Reports*, *121*(3), 294–298.

Adelman, H. S., & Taylor, L. (2012). Mental health in schools: Moving in new directions. *Contemporary School Psychology*, *16*, 9–18.

Benard, B. (2004). *Resiliency: What we have learned*. WestEd.

Bronfenbrenner, U. (1977). Toward an experimental ecology of human development. *American Psychologist*, *32*(7), 513–531. https://doi.org/10.1037/0003-066X.32.7.513

Burns, B. J., Costello, E. J., Angold, A., Tweed, D., Stangl, D., Farmer, E. M., & Erkanli, A. (1995). Children's mental health service use across service sectors. *Health Affairs*, *14*, 147–159. https://dx.doi.org/10.1377/hlthaff.14.3.147

Cicchetti, D., Rogosch, F. A., Lynch, M., & Holt, K. D. (1993). Resilience in maltreated children: Processes leading to adaptive outcome. *Development & Psychopathology*, *5*(4), 629–647. https://dx.doi.org/10.1017/S0954579400006209

Collins, T. A., Dart, E. H., & Arora, P. G. (2019). Addressing the internalizing behavior of students in schools: Applications of the MTSS model. *School Mental Health: A Multidisciplinary Research and Practice Journal*, *11*(2), 191–193. https://doi-org.libproxy.chapman.edu/10.1007/s12310-018-09307-9

Doll, B., & Cummings, J. A. (2008). *Transforming school mental health services: Population-based approaches to promoting the competency and wellness of children*. Corwin Press.

Emmons, R. A., & Stern, R. (2013). Gratitude as a psychotherapeutic intervention. *Journal of Clinical Psychology, 8*, 846–855. https://dx.doi.org/10.1002/jclp.22020

Fredrickson, B. L. (2001). The role of positive emotions in positive psychology: The broaden-and-build theory of positive emotions. *The American Psychologist, 56*(3), 218–226.

Furlong, M. J., Gilman, R., & Huebner, E. S. (2014). *Handbook of positive psychology in schools* (2nd ed.). Routledge/Taylor & Francis Group.

Garmezy, N. (1993). Children in poverty: Resilience despite risk. *Psychiatry, 56*, 127–136.

Gillham, J. E., Reivich, K. J., & Shatté, A. J. (2001). Building optimism and preventing depressive symptoms in children. In E. C. Chang (Ed.), *Optimism and pessimism: Implications for theory, research, and practice* (pp. 301–320). American Psychological Association. https://dx.doi.org/10.1037/10385-014

Gischlar, K. L., Keller-Margulis, M., & Faith, E. L. (2019). Ten years of response to intervention: Trends in the school psychology literature. *Contemporary School Psychology, 23*(3), 201–210. https://doi-org.libproxy.chapman.edu/10.1007/s40688-018-0179-9

Green, A. E., Willging, C. E., Zamarin, K., Dehaiman, L. M., & Ruiloba, P. (2019). Cultivating healing by implementing restorative practices for youth: Protocol for a cluster randomized trial. *International Journal of Educational Research, 93*, 168–176. https://doi-org.libproxy.chapman.edu/10.1016/j.ijer.2018.11.005

Guckenburg, S., Hurley, N., Persson, H., Fronius, T., & Petrosino, A. (2015). *Restorative justice in U.S. schools: Summary findings from interviews with experts*. WestEd.

Gutkin, T. B. (2012). Ecological psychology: Replacing the medical model paradigm for school-based psychological and psychoeducational services. *Journal of Educational and Psychological Consultation, 22*(1–2), 1–20. http://www.tandfonline.com/toc/hepc20/current

Hass, M. (2018). *Interviewing for assessment: A practical guide for school counselors and school psychologists*. John Wiley & Sons.

Horner, R. H., Kincaid, D., Sugai, G., Lewis, T., Eber, L., Barrett, S., Dickey, C. R., Richter, M., Sullivan, E., Boezio, C., Algozzine, B., Reynolds, H., & Johnson, N. (2014). Scaling up school-wide positive behavioral interventions and supports: Experiences of seven states with documented success. *Journal of Positive Behavior Interventions, 16*(4), 197–208.

Luthar, S. S., Cicchetti, D., & Becker, B. (2000). The construct of resilience: A critical evaluation and guidelines for future work. *Child Development, 71*(3), 543–562.

Masten, A. S. (2014). *Ordinary magic: Resilience in development*. Guilford Press.

Masten, A. S., & Curtis, W. J. (2000). Integrating competence and psychopathology: Pathways toward a comprehensive science of adaption in development. *Development and Psychopathology, 12*(3), 529–550. https://dx.doi.org/10.1017/S095457940000314X

Mills, C. W. (1959). *The sociological imagination*. Oxford University Press.

Murphy, J. J. (2013). Student-driven interviewing: Practical strategies for building strength-based interventions. *Communique, 41*(7), 10–12.

Nastasi, B. K. (2004). Meeting the challenges of the future: Integrating public health and public education for mental health promotion. *Journal of Educational & Psychological Consultation, 15*(3 & 4), 295–312.

Pedrotti, J. T., Edwards, L. M., & Lopez, S. J. (2008). Promoting hope: Suggestions for school counselors. *Professional School Counseling, 12*(2), 100–107.

Rutter, M. (2013). Annual research review: Resilience—Clinical implications. *Journal of Child Psychology and Psychiatry, 54*(4), 474–487. https://doi.org/10.1111/j.1469-7610.2012.02615.x

Saleeby, D. (2000). Power in the people: Strengths and hope. *Advances in Social Work, 1*(2), 127–136. https://doi.org/10.18060/18

Seligman, M. P. (2004). *Authentic happiness: Using the new positive psychology to realize your potential for lasting fulfillment*. Free Press.

Sugai, G., Horner, R. H., & Lewis, T. (2009). *School-wide positive behavior support implementers' blueprint and self-assessment*. University of Oregon, OSEP TA-Center on Positive Behavioral Interventions and Supports.

Wachtel, T. (2013). *Defining restorative*. International Institute for Restorative Practices.

Werner, E. E., & Smith, R. S. (2001). *Journeys from childhood to midlife: Risk, resilience, and recovery*. Cornell University.

Wiley, D. C., & Cory, A. C. (2013). *Encyclopedia of school health*. SAGE Publications.

Zehr, H. (1990). *Changing lenses: A new focus for crime and justice*. Herald Press.

2

Background

To better understand how to respond to students' mental health challenges, it is essential to understand what is meant by mental health. This chapter expands on the notion of a public health approach to mental health and multitiered systems of support, discussed in Chapter 1. Then, we discuss how children's mental health is best understood as the interaction of the signs and symptoms of mental health problems and a sense of subjective well-being and include a discussion of the interplay of risk and resilience. This chapter lays the groundwork for later chapters, where we will discuss in detail the skills needed to develop supportive relationships and provide specific guidelines for how teachers can distinguish common but sometimes challenging behaviors from more troubling behaviors that require follow-up.

A Public Health Perspective on Promoting Mental Health

Public health is an attempt by a society to address health problems that affect communities (Holland et al., 1991). Public health has several functions, the first of which is prevention. Examples of actions that prevent physical health problems include the provision of healthy drinking water or adequate sanitation, available to everyone in a community, regardless of their health status. The second function is early intervention

DOI: 10.4324/9780367810269-2

that controls or mitigates the impact of illness, preventing it from becoming worse by addressing substantial risk factors in an early stage of a disease. In the realm of physical health, this might involve early screening for heart disease or programs to help obese people lose weight. The last function is care or cure (Costello & Angold, 2000). Care involves managing chronic problems that do not have a cure to the extent that those affected can maintain a high quality of life despite their illness. Interventions related to care also often attempt to prevent an issue from becoming worse. Diabetes is an example of a disease for which care is vital to maintain quality of life and prevent greater severity. Cure is providing treatment that eliminates the disease and, ideally, returns the person to health, for example, surgery for an operable heart defect or antibiotics for a bacterial infection.

As discussed in Chapter 1, in education, the public health model has often been framed as a multitiered system of support (MTSS). MTSS is a way of organizing and delivering services through three or more tiers. Whether academic, behavioral, or mental health-focused, Tier 1 services, available to all children, focus on facilitating healthy development and preventing problems before they occur (Adelman & Taylor, 2012). Examples of Tier 1 systems include high-quality and responsive academic instruction, frequent positive reinforcement of clear expectations, and delivery of classroom-based programs that teach positive social skills and emotional self-regulation.

Tier 2 supports are focused on students who do not make enough progress with Tier 1 supports. Adelman and Taylor (2012) describe Tier 2 inventions as seeking to "identify, correct, or at least minimize problems as early after their onset as is feasible" (p. 295). Tier 2 interventions might include focused small-group academic instruction for students who need more support than do their peers or psychoeducational groups that provide specific instruction in critical social or organizational skills.

Tier 3 consists of intense and individualized interventions for students who are most in need and have not benefited sufficiently from Tier 2 interventions. For example, much of what occurs in special education programs, in which each child receives an individualized program, might be considered Tier 3 services. Examples include longer-term individual counseling or an individualized behavior intervention plan. Returning to the language of the public health model, Adelman and Taylor (2010) describe Tier 3 as systems of care. Systems of care are interconnected and provide longer-term supports designed to return students with severe or chronic problems to more typical functioning or, in general, provide the care or support that students need to succeed in school despite their challenges.

There are two important examples of the application of MTSS in education. One includes response to intervention (RtI) systems, for which the focus has been mainly on providing evidence-based academic supports and identifying specific learning disabilities (Gischlar et al., 2019). Another example is systems of school-wide positive behavioral supports (SWPBS). Derived from the principles of applied behavior analysis, SWPBS focuses primarily on individual social behaviors and how school environments make those behaviors more or less likely to occur (Sugai & Horner, 2009). Doll (2019) notes that, although discussions of MTSS often focus on the different tiers, the most critical aspects of the framework are the use of universal screening, progress monitoring, and assessment data to prioritize school resources.

As the description of these tiers suggests, in an MTSS approach, the focus moves from individuals, for which treatment is provided to those in most need, to a system that is concerned with the success of the entire school population (Doll et al., 2014; Nastasi, 2004). The public health approach and MTSS also have begun to influence how school-based mental health services are organized. Like RtI and SWPBS, a mental health-focused MTSS framework includes components that promote social and emotional development and well-being for all, minimizes the occurrence of problems, identifies and intervenes with issues when they begin to emerge, and coordinates treatment of severe and chronic problems (Adelman & Taylor, 2010, 2012). Given that SWPBS has long focused on more visible social behaviors, much of the discussion about including a broader range of mental health problems in the scope of SWPBS has focused on how to address less obvious and socially disruptive mental health problems, such as depression and anxiety (Collins et al., 2019; Doll, 2019). Related concerns include inadequate training of SBMH providers and teachers; a lack of collaboration between families, schools, and community partners; poor coordination of available supports and resources; and inadequate implementation of evidence-based practices (Stephan et al., 2015).

There are two dimensions to MTSS approaches to providing mental health supports. One is the services provided, and the other is the intensity of the needs of individual students. Following a public health framework, the services move from universal supports, such as positive school and classroom climates or social-emotional learning programs, to intense individualized support for those with severe or chronic problems.

In terms of delivering mental health supports in an MTSS system, the teacher's role is often one of providing classroom-based universal supports or early identification of mental health problems. In addition, teachers are frequently involved with students with more severe needs at all of the MTSS framework levels. Students who have experienced a significant loss or other traumatic event might approach a teacher before contacting a mental health professional. Although teachers are not trained mental health professionals, they are often "gateway providers," who initiate referrals and facilitate access to services (Stiffman et al., 2004).

As we discussed in Chapter 1, we conceptualize the tiers of an MTSS framework as follows: Tier 1, mental health promotion; Tier 2, mental health prevention for those at risk; Tier 3, specialized care and treatment; and Tier 4, response to crisis. Included in this framework are four actions that are critical for teachers to master: relating, recognizing, responding, and referring. To provide background for these four actions and how they fit into the four components of the MTSS framework, we explore the nature of mental health and the interplay of risk and resilience.

> **Reflection**
>
> - At your school, what policies, programs, or activities exist that you would consider primary prevention?
> - What programs exist that would be considered Tier 2, or secondary prevention?
> - If you have students who seem to need intense services, what is the process for connecting them to those services?

Mental Health: More than the Absence of Problems

Cultures have long had ways of classifying and labeling different kinds of illnesses. With the introduction of the scientific method into medicine in the mid-19th century, accurate diagnosis and classification took on a special significance. Greenspoon and Saflofske (2001) describe diagnosis and classification as the "search for pathological processes or entities so that we can excise them, or otherwise rid the person (or 'host') of them, assuming that their destruction will result in a relative return to normalcy or health" (p. 81).

This approach has come to dominate psychology and how teachers and administrators think about children and their mental health difficulties. When presented with a challenging student, it is not unusual for us to first ask, "What does the child have?" An often upspoken assumption in these statements is that, when these conditions are "corrected," the student will resume a state of normalcy, or "mental health." As Renshaw and Cohen (2014) stated, most research into mental health starts from "a working assumption ... which supposes that decreases in psychological distress are synonymous with—or at least automatically accompanied by—increases in psychological well-being" (p. 320).

There are many limitations to this approach. Even mental health professionals are not very reliable at making diagnoses and categorizing children. For example, in the field trials for the newest edition of the *Diagnostic and Statistical Manual* (DSM-5), the reference book used by psychiatrists and other mental health professionals to diagnose mental health disorders, interrater agreement or reliability was only a little better than chance for common problems, such as depression and generalized anxiety disorder (Freedman et al., 2013). This lack of reliability is not unique to psychiatrists who use the DSM but also is the case for school-based practitioners who use the special education categories in the Individuals with Disabilities Act (Sullivan, Sadeh, & Houri, 2019; Watkins, 2009). Despite this lack of reliability, even among highly trained professionals, it is still common to find educators casually using labels such as *ADD* or *emotionally disturbed* as a kind of shorthand in conversations without understanding how little this actually tells us about how to help children effectively.

In addition to reliability, there are other limitations to the "What does the child have?" approach. Even when accurate, these labels provide limited information about what supports children need (Kamphaus et al., 2013; Timimi, 2014). This approach also focuses our attention exclusively on children's problems and limitations, which can blind us to personal and social strengths that coexist with mental health problems. Not only can these strengths exist alongside difficulties and barriers, but some evidence suggests that strengths are better predictors of functioning later in life than is the absence of emotional and behavioral symptoms (Kohlberg et al., 1972, 1984). These findings suggest that there is more to mental health than merely the absence of problems.

In Chapter 1, we noted that multiple studies over the last several decades have concluded that about 20% of children and youth have a diagnosable mental health disorder. An essential finding of several of these studies is that not all children who meet the criteria for a formal diagnosis have high levels of impairment. In other words, having enough symptoms to meet the criteria for a disorder does not mean that a child is struggling at home or school or even feels bad about his or her life. When impairment is considered, the 20% figure dropped to 11% in one study (Burns et al., 1995). In another study (Shaffer et al., 1996), 32.8% of children met the criteria for a DSM diagnosis but only 21%, when mild impairment was used as a criterion and only about 5%, when researchers set the benchmark at severe impairment.

These findings do not diminish the need for prevention and intervention for mental health problems—as even 12% represents a large number of struggling children—but they point to something other than the presence or absence of psychiatric symptoms that influence children's mental health. Given these and other findings, researchers have pushed back against the notion that mental health is simply the automatic result of the removal of the symptoms or illness (Greenspoon & Saflofske, 2001). Criticisms of such definitions of mental health go back many decades (Greenspoon & Saflofske, 2001), and the development of positive psychology (Seligman, 2004) has given weight to the perspective that a comprehensive definition of mental health should consider positive indicators of mental health as well as the signs and symptoms of mental health challenges. This broader framework moves us away from the question of, "What does the child have?" to "What is going on in the child's life?" The focus shifts from diagnosis to curiosity.

One model of the integration of problems and positive indicators of mental health is the dual-factor model of mental health (e.g., Antaramian et al., 2010; Greenspoon & Saflofske, 2001; Lyons et al., 2013; Suldo & Shaffer, 2008; Suldo et al., 2016). Proponents of a dual-factor model argue that a comprehensive definition of mental health should include two aspects: the weight of problems in children's lives (with a focus that is not necessarily on a diagnostic category) and subjective well-being.

Subjective well-being is a way for researchers to operationalize happiness (Suldo & Shaffer, 2008). Subjective well-being has three related but distinct components: global life satisfaction, positive affect, and negative affect (Suldo et al., 2016). Life satisfaction is how one thinks about the overall quality of one's life (Suldo & Shaffer, 2008). Most studies include questions such as those below, taken from the Brief Multidimensional Student's Life Satisfaction Scale (Seligson et al., 2003). Children respond to these questions on a 7-point Likert scale, with answers that range from delighted to mostly satisfied or strongly agree to strongly disagree.

1. My life is going well.
2. My life is just right.
3. I would like to change many things in my life.

4. I wish I had a different kind of life.
5. I have a good life.
6. I have what I want in life.
7. My life is better than most kids.

Although life satisfaction is the cognitive component of subjective well-being, or how one thinks about the quality of one's life, the emotional aspect of subjective well-being is how often one experiences positive and negative emotions (Diener et al., 2009). In studies that investigate the dual-factor model of mental health, the emotional aspect of subjective well-being has most often been assessed using the Positive and Negative Affectivity Scale (PANAS; Watson et al., 1988). The PANAS asks children and youth (as well as adults) to rate the following list of feeling words on a scale from 1 = very slightly or not at all, 2 = a little, 3 = moderately, 4 = quite a bit, or 5 = extremely or very much:

- interested
- distressed
- excited
- upset
- strong
- guilty
- scared
- hostile
- enthusiastic
- proud
- irritable
- alert
- ashamed
- inspired
- nervous
- determined
- attentive
- jittery
- active
- afraid

These emotions are divided into negative affect or emotional states and positive affect. Positive affect (PA) reflects how much someone feels energized, alert, and enthusiastic. Low PA levels are characterized by sadness and lethargy (Watson et al., 1988). Negative Affect (NA) represents distress and the experience of negative moods or emotions, for example, distressed, scared, irritable, and nervous.

Taken together, life satisfaction and the experience of positive and negative affect seem to provide a reliable and valid snapshot of someone's subjective experience of life. This subjective experience is related to a variety of possible psychosocial and physical health outcomes, including reduced thoughts of suicide (Chang & Sanna, 2001), better physical health, increased longevity (Diener & Chan, 2011), greater likelihood of staying in college, and even the higher possibility of marriage among adults. Further findings from multiple research studies suggest that subjective well-being has a distinct contribution to how well someone does in school and life. In other words, how successful children are in our classrooms and communities is not merely the result of how many (or few) symptoms they have or how much (or little) distress they experience but also is significantly influenced by their subjective sense of well-being.

Studies of children and youth in elementary school, middle school, high school, and college that use the dual-factor model of mental health have consistently identified four groups within a range of mental health (e.g., Antaramian et al., 2010; Greenspoon & Saflofske, 2001; Lyons et al., 2013; Reshaw & Cohen, 2014; Suldo & Shaffer, 2008; Suldo et al., 2016). These studies suggest that about two-thirds of the populations studied can be regarded as having "complete mental health." This group has few, if any, signs of psychopathology and high levels of subjective well-being (high levels of life satisfaction, frequent positive emotions, and relatively few negative emotions). About 15% of the population has high levels of psychopathology and low levels of subjective well-being. This group has been labeled "troubled." This figure roughly matches the number of children identified as having an identifiable disorder and significant impairment by the studies discussed above. These two groups, troubled and complete mental health, fit how most of us imagine any given classroom, school, or community might be divided.

The remaining two groups are considered "vulnerable" or "content." The vulnerable group, according to researchers, include about 15% of those studied. Members of this group have few traditional signs of psychopathology, yet have low levels of subjective well-being. The final group is considered content. This group consists of those who score high on traditional measures of psychopathology but, surprisingly, also have relatively high levels of subjective well-being.

These differences have practical implications for children's lives. For example, symptomatic students who have higher subjective well-being tend to be more connected to peers and teachers and satisfied with their social relationships (Suldo & Shaffer, 2008; Suldo et al., 2016). This finding suggests that, despite their challenges, they can make friends and recruit adult support. Simultaneously, students who had low subjective well-being but few, if any, signs of psychopathology have less academic motivation and view school as less important than do students with higher levels of subjective well-being. In other words, this group did not have apparent signs of mental health problems but were still unhappy and less connected to their school.

Reflection

- Thinking of the dual-factor model of mental health discussed above, can you think of children you know who would fall into the categories of (a) complete mental health, (b) troubled, (c) vulnerable, and (d) content?
- Considering the students you have worked with who seemed to have lots of problems, what assets or strengths did they have? What difference did those strengths make in their lives?

The Interplay of Risk and Resilience

Subjective well-being is an essential indicator of mental health but does not tell us specifically what leads children to think positively about their lives or experience more positive emotions. To better understand what underlies the interplay of subjective well-being and psychosocial difficulties, it is essential to understand the notions of risk and resilience. Perhaps because it fits with the deeply held American narrative of being able to "pull yourself up by your bootstraps," resilience is often discussed as something remarkable that happens with only special children, mainly through their own efforts (Masten, 2001). We admire stories of overcoming the odds and often attribute those successes to grit, determination, or other individual qualities. Yet, as we discussed in Chapter 1, resilience is both an everyday phenomenon and the result of dynamic systems that Masten (2001) has described as "ordinary magic." They include, first and foremost, close relationships. In the context of close relationships, other factors, such as problem-solving, self-regulation, sense of personal agency, and hope for the future, can develop (Masten, 2014; Werner, 1992).

Resilience exists only in relationship to adversity, and, as such, it is essential to understand the nature of risk or adversity. The most well-documented studies of risk have used the concept of adverse childhood experiences (ACEs). In the original ACEs study (Felitti et al., 1998), 13,494 adults who had completed a medical evaluation at a large HMO in Southern California were sent a survey that had items pertaining to whether they had experienced any of several different types of different ACEs. The first wave of research participants was asked about seven kinds of negative experiences, including psychological, physical, or sexual abuse; violence against mothers or stepmothers; or living with household members who were substance abusers, mentally ill or suicidal, or ever imprisoned. Later waves of the research added physical and emotional neglect and parental separation as ACEs (Petruccelli et al., 2019).

One important finding was that these ACEs were remarkably common. Of the 9,508 people who responded to the survey, over half had experienced at least one of the above negative childhood experiences, and 6% had experienced four or more ACEs. The researchers also found that the more exposure someone had to ACEs, the higher the risk was for various negative outcomes in adulthood. These included adverse psychosocial outcomes, such as suicidality, substance abuse, and unwanted pregnancy, but also medical problems, such as heart disease, cancer, emphysema, hepatitis, and even bone fractures (Felitti et al., 1998).

It is noteworthy that the population surveyed in the original ACEs study was predominately White, relatively well educated, economically middle to upper-middle class, and insured. A later study (Cronholm et al., 2015) developed the understanding of the ACEs by gathering data from a racially and socioeconomically diverse urban population. The researchers expanded the seven categories of the original ACE survey to include items related to "community dysfunction." These additional items included witnessing violence, feeling discriminated against, living in an unsafe neighborhood, being bullied, and living in foster care.

Among the 1,784 respondents in this study, which used this expanded definition of ACEs, over 72% had at least one of the original ACEs, and 63.4% had a least one of the expanded ACEs. Almost 50% had at least one of both. Although this study did not look at the relationship between community dysfunction and specific health outcomes, the results suggest that, in less economically advantaged and racially diverse communities, ACEs may be considerably more common than the already high levels found in the original ACEs study.

Later studies have confirmed the relationship between ACEs and negative psychosocial and physical outcomes (Petruccelli et al., 2019). Much of the research on ACEs has contributed to the argument that screening for and identifying risk is essential in providing care. In medical settings such as the one where the original ACEs study was conducted, it became clear that, to effectively address many chronic physical problems, it was also necessary to address the underlying psychosocial issues. In regard to the findings of the ACEs study, Hari (2018) stated, "There's a house fire inside many of us ... and we're concentrating on the smoke" (p. 136). If this is true for the adults who seek care in medical settings, it is undoubtedly true for the children in our classrooms.

In the context of resilience, it is important to note that many ACEs seem to disrupt these protective systems. For example, abuse disrupts attachment and close relationships. It also diminishes a sense of personal agency and hope, which, in turn, erodes self-regulation and self-direction. In different ways, having a caregiver absent, whether due to mental illness or imprisonment, has a similarly negative effect.

Although ACEs seem to be incredibly common, it is important to remind ourselves that research on resilience gives us hope that many, if not most, children can overcome these challenges to succeed in life. Further, research on resilience can provide us with guidance on how teachers and educators can help many children who experience adverse experiences and are at risk for negative developmental outcomes.

A seminal longitudinal study of resilience conducted by Werner and Smith (1982, 2001) followed a cohort of children from birth to 32 years of age. Most were of Japanese, Pilipino, and Hawaiian descent and had parents who had not graduated from high school. Many of these children had multiple risk factors, starting at birth with complications during pregnancy, labor, or delivery. Yet, despite these and later risk factors, such as poor reading skills, delinquency, early pregnancy, and mental health problems, one-third of these children grew up to be young adults who "loved well, worked well, played well, and expected well" (Werner, 1992, p. 263).

Several factors made a difference in the lives of these children, but most important to our discussion of schools and teachers are supportive ties with grandparents, older siblings, teachers, or other supportive adults and participation in school or community activities, whereby children's competency and sense of self-efficacy were recognized and encouraged. Benard (2004) stated that protective environments in homes, schools, or communities are those that provide caring relationships; clear and positive expectations; and opportunities to take part, contribute, and give back. Much of what we discuss in later chapters draw from these findings.

Reflection

- What sources of resilience do the students in your classroom have? Think of both social and personal assets.
- What can you do to encourage resilience in yourself and your students?

Takeaways

- Comprehensive mental health services are best organized using a public health model that includes mental health promotion, mental health prevention for those at risk, specialized care and treatment, and response to crisis.
- Mental health is a function of the presence or absence of problems or psychopathology and subjective well-being.
- Adverse childhood events, such as abuse, are remarkably common and have long-term physical and mental health effects.
- Resilience is the ability to bounce back from adverse events. It comprises close relationships, problem solving, self-regulation, a sense of personal agency, and hope for the future. Positive relationships are key.

References

Adelman, H. S., & Taylor, L. (2010). *Mental health in schools: Engaging learners, preventing problems, and improving schools*. Corwin.

Adelman, H. S., & Taylor, L. (2012). Mental health in schools: Moving in new directions. *Contemporary School Psychology, 16*, 9–18.

Antaramian, S. P., Huebner, E. S., Hills, K. J., & Valois, R. F. (2010). A dual-factor model of mental health: Toward a more comprehensive understanding of youth functioning. *American Journal of Orthopsychiatry, 80*, 462–472. https://doi.org/10.1111/j.1939-0025.2010.01049.x

Benard, B. (2004). *Resiliency: What we have learned*. WestEd.

Burns, B. J., Costello, E. J., Angold, A., Tweed, D., Stangl, D., Farmer, E. M., & Erkanli, A. (1995). Children's mental health service use across service sectors. *Health Affairs, 14*, 147–159.

Chang, E. C., & Sanna, L. J. (2001). Optimism, pessimism, and positive and negative affectivity in middle-aged adults: A test of a cognitive-affective model of psychological adjustment. *Psychology and Aging, 16*, 524–531.

Collins, T. A., Dart, E. H., & Arora, P. G. (2019). Addressing the internalizing behavior of students in schools: Applications of the MTSS model.

School Mental Health: A Multidisciplinary Research and Practice Journal, 11(2), 191–193.

Costello, E. J., & Angold, A. (2000, January 1). Developmental psychopathology and public health: Past, present, and future. Development and Psychopathology, 12(4), 599–618.

Cronholm, P. F., Forke, C. M., Wade, R., Bair-Merritt, M. H., Davis, M., Harkins-Schwarz, M., Pachter, L. M , & Fein, J. A. (2015). Adverse childhood experiences: Expanding the concept of adversity. American Journal of Preventive Medicine, 49(3), 354–361.

Diener, E., & Chan, M. Y. (2011). Happy people live longer: Subjective well-being contributes to health and longevity. Applied Psychology: Health and Well-Being, 3(1), 1–43.

Diener, E., Scollon, C. N., & Lucas, R. E. (2009). The evolving concept of subjective well-being: The multifaceted nature of happiness. In E. Diener (Ed.), Assessing well-being: The collected works of ed diener (pp. 67–100). Springer.

Doll, B. (2019). Addressing student internalizing behavior through multi-tiered system of support. School Mental Health, 2, 290–293.

Doll, B., Brehm, K., & Zucker, S. (2014). Resilient classrooms, second edition: Creating healthy environments for learning. The Guilford Press.

Felitti, V. J., Anda, R. F., Nordenberg, D., Williamson, D. F., Spitz, A. M., Edwards, V., Koss, M. P., & Marks, J. S. (1998). Relationship of childhood abuse and household dysfunction to many of the leading causes of death in adults. The adverse childhood experiences (ACEs) study. American Journal of Preventive Medicine, 14(4), 245–258.

Freedman, R., Lewis, D., Michels, R., Pine, D., Schultz, S., Tamminga, C., Gabbard, G., Gau, S., Javitt, D., Oquendo, M., Shrout, P., Vieta, E. & Yager, J. (2013). The initial field trials of DSM-5: New blooms and old thorns. American Journal of Psychiatry, 170(1), 1–5. https://doi.org/10.1176/appi.ajp.2012.12091189

Gischlar, K. L., Keller-Margulis, M., & Faith, E. L. (2019). Ten years of response to intervention: Trends in the school psychology literature. Contemporary School Psychology, 23(3), 201–210.

Greenspoon, P. J., & Saklofske, D. H. (2001). Toward an integration of subjective well-being and psychopathology. Social Indicators Research, 54, 81–108. https://doi.org/10.1023/A:1007219227883

Hari, J. (2018). *Lost connections: Why you're depressed and how to find hope*. Bloomsbury.

Holland, W. W., Detels, R., Knox, G., Fitzsimons, B., & Gardner, L. (1991). *Oxford textbook of public health*. Oxford University Press.

Kamphaus, R. W., Dowdy, E., Kim, S., & Chin, J. (2013). Diagnosis, classification, and screening systems. In D. H. Saklofske, V. L. Schwan, & C. R. Reynolds (Eds.), *The Oxford handbook of child psychological assessment* (pp. 182–201). Oxford University Press. https://doi.org/10.1093/oxfordhb/9780199796304.013.0009

Kohlberg, L., Ricks, D., & Snarey, J. (1972). The predictability of adult mental health from childhood behavior. In B. B. Wolman (Ed.), *Manual of child psychopathology* (pp. 1217–1284). New York, NY: McGraw-Hill.

Kohlberg, L., Ricks, D., & Snarey, J. (1984). Childhood development as a predictor of adaptation in adulthood. *Genetic Psychology Monographs, 110*, 91–172.

Lyons, M., Huebner, E., & Hills, K. (2013). The dual-factor model of mental health: A short-term longitudinal study of school-related outcomes. *Social Indicators Research, 114*(2), 549–565.

Masten, A. S. (2001). Ordinary magic: Resilience processes in development. *American Psychologist, 56*(3), 227–238.

Masten, A. S. (2014). *Ordinary magic: Resilience in development*. Guilford Press.

Nastasi, B. K. (2004). Meeting the challenges of the future: Integrating public health and public education for mental health promotion. *Journal of Educational & Psychological Consultation, 15*(3 & 4), 295–312.

Petruccelli, K., Davis, J., & Berman, T. (2019). Adverse childhood experiences and associated health outcomes: A systematic review and meta-analysis. *Child Abuse & Neglect, 97*, 2–31.

Renshaw, T. L., & Cohen, A. S. (2014). Life satisfaction as a distinguishing indicator of college student functioning: Further validation of the two-continua model of mental health. *Social Indicators Research, 117*(1), 319–335.

Seligman, M. P. (2004). *Authentic happiness: Using the new positive psychology to realize your potential for lasting fulfillment*. New York: Free Press.

Seligson, J., Huebner, E., & Valois, R. (2003). Preliminary validation of the brief multidimensional students' life satisfaction scale (BMSLSS). *Social Indicators Research: An International and Interdisciplinary Journal for Quality-of-Life Measurement, 61*(2), 121.

Shaffer, D., Fisher, P., Canino, G., Regier, D., Dulcan, M. K., Davies, M., Placentini, J., Schwab-Store, M. E., Lahey, B. B., Bourdon, K., Jensen, P. S., & Brid, H. R. (1996). The NIMH diagnostic interview schedule for children version 2.3 (DISC-2.3) : Description, acceptability, prevalence rates, and performance in the MECA study : Epidemiology of child and adolescent mental disorders. *Journal of the American Academy of Child and Adolescent Psychiatry, 35*(7), 865–877.

Stephan, S. H., Sugai, G., Lever, N., & Connors, E. (2015). Strategies for integrating mental health into schools via a multitiered system of support. *Child and Adolescent Psychiatric Clinics of North America, 24*(2), 211–231.

Stiffman, A. R., Pescosolido, B., & Cabassa, L. J. (2004). Building a model to understand youth service access: The gateway provider model. *Mental Health Services Research, 6*(4), 189–198.

Sugai, G., & Horner, R. H. (2009). Responsiveness-to-intervention and school-wide positive behavior supports: Integration of multitiered system approaches. *Exceptionality, 17*(4), 223–237.

Suldo, S. M., & Shaffer, E. J. (2008). Looking beyond psychopathology: The dual-factor model of mental health in youth. *School Psychology Review, 37*(1), 52–68.

Suldo, S. M., Thalji-Raitano, A., Kiefer, S. M., & Ferron, J. M. (2016). Conceptualizing high school students' mental health through a dual-factor model. *School Psychology Review, 45*(4), 434–457.

Sullivan, A. L., Sadeh, S., & Houri, A. K. (2019). Are school psychologists' special education eligibility decisions reliable and unbiased? A multi-study experimental investigation. *Journal of School Psychology, 77*, 90–109.

Timimi, S. (2014). No more psychiatric labels: Why formal psychiatric diagnostic systems should be abolished. *International Journal of Clinical and Health Psychology, 14*, 208–215. https://doi.org/10.1016/j.ijchp.2014.03.004

Watkins, M. W. (2009). Errors in diagnostic decision-making and clinical judgment. In T. B. Gutkin & C. R. Reynolds (Eds.), *The handbook of school psychology* (4th ed., pp. 210–229). Wiley.

Watson, D., & Clark, L. A., & Tellegen, A. (1988). Positive and Negative Affect Schedule. *PsycTESTS*.

Werner, E. E. (1992). The children of Kauai: Resiliency and recovery in adolescence and adulthood. *Journal of Adolescent Health*, *13*, 262–268.

Werner, E. E., & Smith, R. S. (1982). *Vulnerable, but invincible: A longitudinal study of resilient children and youth*. McGraw-Hill.

Werner, E. E., & Smith, R. S. (2001). *Journeys from childhood to midlife: Risk, resilience, and recovery*. Cornell University Press.

3

The First R

Relate

Humans are fundamentally social, and, thus, supportive connections with others are an essential factor in promoting mental health. As we noted in our discussion of resilience in Chapter 2, supportive relationships are key in the process of recovery from adversity (Arvidson et al., 2011; Cozolino, 2013; Masten, 2014). As many schools work toward implementing multitiered systems of support (MTSS), teachers are incorporating classroom engagement strategies with behavioral, emotional, and cognitive components (Fredricks et al., 2004). Simple acts, such as greeting students at the door or modeling how to articulate feelings, are becoming more common. Unlike using a traditional hierarchical model of classroom management, building a classroom community centered on relationships involves holistic classroom designs. Here students' socioemotional health is valued and understood as directly connected to academic learning.

Relationship-centered classrooms require safe environments that promote social connections, are culturally responsive, and involve student choice, while still positioning the teacher as the adult authority. Because schools are micro-communities where children learn how to be in the world outside of their families, spending classroom time to build relationships would appear to be common sense. Yet, it takes thoughtfulness, intentionality, and discipline on the part of teaching professionals. This chapter focuses on what it means to plan for, enact, and expand relationships of professional care with students, their families, and their communities.

What Kinds of Relationships Do We Need in Schools and Why?

Before getting to the "how to" of relationships, it is helpful to first consider why relationships are central to effective teaching and to supporting positive mental health. Brain science offers an essential perspective on the necessity of positive relationships for human learning. It also helps teachers to identify their role in a child's social and emotional development more clearly.

As you read, consider using this information about the brain as a way to understand and discuss emotions and relationships with students.[1] Information about the brain and its functions can be adjusted to be developmentally appropriate, allowing for students' understanding of their brains to deepen as they grow older. Learning about how the brain influences how people think, feel, and learn can empower students by enhancing their self-awareness and sense of self-control, becoming a reference for conversations and collective reflections throughout the school year.

Suppose students use physical harm or unkind words to solve a conflict on the playground. In response, teachers can debrief students by referencing those parts of the brain that contributed to those actions and what parts of their brain they needed to strengthen instead. These conversations can become an important first step for students to develop self-mastery and independence as they begin to understand their actions and what they need to do differently. We argue that often, if not most of the time, what children need is such a situation to be better connected to their peers or teachers.

The Brain Science of Relationships Explained Quickly

Lewis and colleagues (2001) explain that the human brain has three key structures, which have developed separately over time. These different structures or "sub-brains" coordinate with each other, although not perfectly, as their differences are not always entirely compatible. The *reptilian brain* is the oldest part of the brain, emerging early in our evolution. It controls basic and essential physical functions, such as breathing, swallowing, heartbeat, visual tracking, and reactions to noise. As Lewis et al. state, the reptilian brain is "steeped in the physiology of survival" (p. 22). Essentially, it directs the functions of our physical body that keep us alive. Although this part of the brain is critical to survival, it has a limited repertoire of basic emotions, such as fear and aggression, but an important influence on mental health, especially anxiety and worry.

The *limbic brain* is the part of the brain that makes us mammals. It is the part of the brain that guides social connections and actions, such as caring for offspring and family members, forming social groups, and playing with others. These behaviors are fundamental for our survival as social animals. More will be said later about the limbic brain, as this is the part of the brain that is the basis for our need for connection, belonging, encouragement, and positive communication.

The newest structure of the brain, the *neocortex*, is what makes us distinct from other mammals. It allows us to set goals, prepare, strategize, plan, problem solve, use language, and entertain abstract concepts. For all its benefits, however, this part of the brain must work, at times, awkwardly and inefficiently with the older parts of the brain to make decisions and take effective actions. Therefore, these newer abilities build upon and are influenced by the older, more basic reactions of the reptilian and limbic structures, most often unconsciously. For example, the limbic system is responsible for attachment and most emotions, while the neocortex draws upon language to express them. These two structures of our brain work together to infuse emotion with words and express our conceptual understandings. If not, we would simply sound like robots as we recited facts and logical arguments (Think Spock from *Star Trek*, although even he had moments of humanness when his underdeveloped Vulcan limbic system was activated.).

More about the Limbic Brain

The limbic brain typically draws upon memories and the emotions associated with those remembered events to understand the world. This understanding is connected to our identities through embodied cultural experiences. This interaction of memory, feelings, and identity makes our reality (or realities) subjective (Lewis et al., 2001). These networks of emotional memories are fluid (and not necessarily "truthful") and are based on the quality of the prior relationships that people had in their lives. For students, the most important relationships are with parents and other caregivers. This history means that students arrive at school on the first day with a sense of how relationships should work, for better or worse. The good news is that our neural pathways can grow and take us in new directions. Thus, regardless of a child's prior relationship history, positive relationships can have an impact on the brain through a process referred to as *limbic revision* (Lewis et al., 2001).

From infancy, a child's connection to another human being is essential to his or her survival. The limbic system of the brain exists primarily to read the emotions of other mammals. When this exchange of emotional information is mutual, it is referred to as limbic resonance (Lewis et al., 2001). Limbic resonance between children and their caregivers, combined with a child's temperament, creates a child's early personhood. This foundation provides young children with a sense of confidence and trust in others, making it more likely that children will develop supportive, secure relationships with others at school and in the community. Ideally, parents are responsive to their children's needs and teach them, through ongoing engagement with patience and compassion, that their needs have value and that their mistakes are part of life. This reciprocal relationship sets up an expectation of a child's earliest way of being in the world, as they are "limbically known," because someone has listened profoundly and communicated to them that their needs matter (Lewis et al., 2001).

Of course, not all children have favorable early life experiences. Fortunately, schools, especially teachers and other adults, provide children with opportunities to learn to know themselves through interactions with others outside of their family. In this way, positive and supportive relationships outside of the home can help children to stabilize themselves by affirming participation in social groups in their schools and communities or even online. In the absence of positive early connections, however, students are more reliant on teachers and others to provide the support necessary to develop healthy skills and habits through a process of social connection and subsequent limbic regulation. Although teachers may worry that a child may be relying on them too much for healthy role modeling and interaction, this is required for the brain to rewire itself to trust others and for the teaching and learning process to work. Over time, a sense of greater security and trust will develop, leading to a sense of independence. This sense of independence does not necessarily happen quickly, and sometimes it will take more than a supportive relationship with a teacher to help. Still, day-to-day, positive relationships are a powerful antidote to many of the stresses outside of school and are key to positive mental health.

As noted, this limbic revision happens when a person is truly known by another. This is how the relationship becomes more powerful than any information taught; in fact, it is the only thing that can teach someone how to transform. Without the relationship, emotional balance cannot occur, and children may find themselves without the capacity to bounce back from stress. Sometimes, even minor stress can feel devastating to their well-being. This is because the amygdala, a structure within the limbic system, will immediately override all other brain systems as a form of protection when faced with a perceived threat, typically through fight, flight, or freeze behaviors (Lewis et al., 2001). Healthy relationships developed through intentional and carefully led, daily practices in which teachers and students are invested in working together can prevent the amygdala's unnecessary triggering. To accomplish this, it takes mindful planning and a particular outlook on relationships and pedagogy, which are discussed next.

What Limbic Revision Looks Like in the Classroom

Many years ago, when I (Amy) was teaching first grade, a new student arrived. Lalo (pseudonym) had come to our U.S. West Coast farming community from Mexico. According to his older brother, a 20-year-old man who served as his guardian, they had left their dying mother to seek work in the United States (U.S.). They had walked the entire way to the U.S. to get jobs in the fields and to send money home for medical care.

Lalo had never attended school before and was rightfully confused by immersion into a brand-new environment. Even though nearly all of his classmates were Mexican immigrants themselves and the majority of instruction occurred in Spanish, the circumstances proved to be overwhelmingly stressful for Lalo. Lalo often resorted to hitting, kicking, and choking classmates when he became frustrated. He also would repeatedly run toward the chain link fence that surrounded our school and try to climb the fence to run home. Because the fence was quite tall (due to the fact that our school was located on a busy street), we were fearful for his safety. Although our class's instructional aide, Ms. Lupe, and I felt a great deal of sympathy for Lalo, other parents were telling us that their children did not feel safe around him and no longer wanted to come to school. We got to work immediately on a Student Study Team meeting to see what we could offer Lalo in terms of support.

With the permission of our wise principal and community social work team, the decision was made to modify Lalo's school day from a full day to a half day until we could get his behavior to change. Our goal was to make sure that the half day of school was a positive experience; we wanted Lalo to feel as welcome and as safe as possible. Ms. Lupe was next to him all day, assisting him with his work, helping him to make friends, sitting with him on the carpet during whole group lessons, and shadowing him at recess. As Lalo felt more known by us (Ms. Lupe, the other students, and me), he began to see that we were all rooting for his success. He knew this because we were conscious to point out the concrete positive contributions that he was making to our community, making him feel seen and understood. Over time, the negative behaviors subsided, and Lalo began to learn and make friends. The limbic resonance that we had patiently created gave him the ability to settle in and see himself as a valued member of our classroom.

Reflection

- Have you had an experience in which having a positive relationship with a student seemed to make an important difference in how they functioned at school? What changed over time? What did you do to make the relationship positive?
- How have supportive relationships made you a better teacher? Person?

Preparing to Relate: What to Think about and Do before Meeting Students and Families

One prominent example of a pedagogy that views learning as fundamentally about relationships is the Reggio Emilia approach for children 0–6 years old (Edwards et al., 1998). Schools guided by this philosophy offer important suggestions for how to design a classroom grounded in human connection. The key elements of the Reggio Emilia approach to teaching and learning include: (1) an enduring image of the child as competent, (2) a classroom environment that serves as a "third teacher," (3) teachers and students who co-research the world as their curriculum through a project-based approach to learning, (4) ongoing observation and documentation of that research to reflect and plan where to go next, and (5) an acknowledgment that children have at least 100 "languages" that they can use to express their knowledge (e.g., conversation, dance, painting, block building).

What this philosophy looks like in practice is profound. Class meetings are held each morning, in which the children sing songs, celebrate birthdays, and share stories about their lives, thus engaging their limbic brains in the process of making and maintain relationships. They would then begin the day's work, including small-group investigations with their teachers, block-building projects, painting, dramatic play, and more. Reconvening in late morning meetings, children and teachers share their work from various centers, get feedback on where they could take their painting or block structure next, and reflect on what they had done, thereby developing the functions of the neocortex. Students might work with the teachers and their peers to determine new investigations based on their curiosities, a process that values their interests and makes them feel "seen" by others. These activities take place in a social environment that facilitates the limbic resonance discussed above. Cognitive learning takes place within supportive relationships.

Observing a learning environment in which relationships are valued highlights the need for intentionality in building relationships in the classroom. Being intentional about creating connections before instruction, in the moment of instruction, and after instruction can bring limbic resonance, regulation, and revision to life in a classroom. In other words, if teachers can enact practices that foreground relationships consistent with philosophies and intentions that see them as integral, the classroom environment is more easily understood, trusted, and engaged in by students.

Before Instruction: Building Relationships with Students

Teachers need to identify and make transparent their underlying assumptions about how school is supposed to be and what learning should look like in their classrooms even before meeting their class. In other words, what is their role as a teacher? What is the role of the students? What counts as knowledge, and what is its purpose? What does it mean to be in school? What is the purpose of school? The answers to these questions can guide the rest of a teacher's planning because it anchors practice in an explicit philosophy consistent with their intentions. In this book, we argue that healthy relationships should be at the center of the answers to these questions.

The Reggio Emilia teachers hold an overarching worldview of *the image of the child as capable* (Edwards et al., 1998). Many U.S. teachers will understand this phrase to mean taking a strengths-based approach to the students in their care. That is, they highlight the gifts that students bring to the classroom and develop their potential from there. Teachers with this mindset adopt a curious rather than a judgmental stance about children's socioemotional and academic development, much in line with the *stance of not knowing*, discussed in Chapter 2.

Reggio Emilia teachers can translate this philosophy into concrete practices that put classroom relationships front and center (Edwards et al., 1998). For example, teachers immersed in the Reggio Emilia approach would say that one of their primary responsibilities is to ask students questions rather than provide them with answers. They value their students' theories (even if they are different from conventional/adult ones) because they trust children to rearrange their thinking across an investigation and their lifespan as new information arises. The assumption is that children have something unique to offer a democratic society and that their voice and point of view matter. Therefore, it is necessary to co-research the world, bringing both the children's and the adults' points of view into dialogue. Through a project-based approach, teachers document that work, reflect on it, and build on it across time with their students. A pedagogical approach of co-researching the world through projects keeps the teacher and the children present in the pursuit of knowledge.

The idea that children can express what they know through 100 languages means that multiple forms of representation are invited and accepted as evidence and expressions of learning (Edwards et al., 1998). K–12 teachers in the U.S.

might recognize that idea as similar to a universal design for learning (Meyer et al., 2014). By documenting (1) instructional and informal conversations, (2) children's observations around activities in the classroom environment (which serves as a "teacher" in and of itself), and (3) inviting peers and the community to comment and participate in investigations directly or vicariously, knowledge becomes collective consciousness (Davis et al., 2015).

Another Reggio Emilia principle that requires intention and that is addressed before the students arrive is the physical classroom environment. Reggio Emilia teachers often talk about how the room needs to be "read" so that the children and visitors can immediately understand how it functions (Edwards et al., 1998). For example, as soon as someone walks through the door of a preschool, they are greeted with a wall hanging with photos of each child and their family that announces "who lives in this space." Classroom spaces are clearly delineated using furniture cues—four chairs at the clay table means four people can sit there—and the gathering space where class meetings are held are often in the center of the room as a way of communicating the value of community dialogue. All non-child-created objects, such as furniture and toys, are neutral in color, and natural objects, like rocks and leaves, are used as learning tools as often as possible. The thinking is that the color should come from the work that the children create and a philosophical stance that children have a right to engage with materials that are beautiful and useful. The overall effect is a calm, welcoming, and orderly room in which children have what they need to accomplish preschool's vital work.

Teachers in the K–12 world cannot just mimic a Reggio Emilia classroom, although they certainly can be inspired by it. Instead, they need to think about the kinds of relationships that they want to create, considering the specific developmental, cultural, historical, linguistic, and political contexts in the communities where they work. Teachers should ask themselves critical questions and develop personal practices that are consistent with their intentions.

Reflection

Consider discussing with a colleague one or more of the following questions:

- What is my personal view of children's role in society? How does this connect to societal norms of children and the role that they play in a democracy before being eligible to vote? What harmonies and tensions might exist here, and how might I plan for that? How do these views inform the teacher-student relationship I need to create?
- Search online for some images of classroom spaces, in the Reggio tradition and otherwise. What pedagogical philosophies are communicated in these spaces? How will you communicate your values through the physical design of your classroom? How does the classroom design have an impact on how children will interact with you and each other in the space?
- Consider your personal philosophy toward teaching and learning. Then audit your actions in the lessons you teach. How closely aligned are your intentions with your practice? How are the children receiving and interpreting these messages? How does their response inform your understanding of your relationship with them?
- How will children be invited/allowed to express what they have learned in your classroom? Do they have the appropriate materials to communicate this knowledge in the classroom and outside of it? How does this have an impact on how you understand them as people? How does this affect how they think and feel toward each other?
- What counts as pedagogy in your class? Who determines what is learned? How is that learning connecting to the lived experiences of your students? What will be the impact of that learning on the child, the family, and the community at large? How does this facilitate healthy intrapersonal and interpersonal relationships inside and outside of the classroom?

Regardless of how you answered the questions above, think about whether your orientations were guided by the goal of foregrounding relationships as the cornerstone of learning. If so, what kinds of relationships can you expect to create using your plan? If not, what might need to be restructured? Although there may be multiple constraints on our work, we all have the ability and, frankly, must make time to talk, listen, reflect, and know each other in meaningful ways that go beyond, yet may include and be grounded in, academic learning. We are creating a microsystem for the students in our care, and this must be done with purposeful intention. Planning matters not just because we now live in an era in which the vision is MTSS in all schools but because our and our students' brains demand it for a thriving existence within and beyond the classroom.

> **Reflection**
>
> - What do you currently do to build relationships with students?
> - How does your classroom environment enhance relationships?

Beginning Relationships with Families

Children come to schools as members of families and communities. Teachers, thus, also must have intention when it comes to building relationships with the other adults in their students' worlds. These people are your *partners*. As Bronfenbrenner (1979) states, "A child's ability to learn to read in the primary grades may depend no less on how he is taught than on the existence and nature of ties between the school and the home" (p. 3). When teachers think about parents, extended family, neighbors, clergy, coaches, afterschool care providers, and other mesosystem-related adults in a way that implies their co-solidarity in supporting the child, they are less alone in both the celebrations of students' success and the challenges that come with particular moments in a student's life. Having the perspectives of others who care equally about the child is also helpful in that it may provide new pathways to solutions or perspectives on a classroom issue that a teacher is not necessarily privy to on their own.

One simple way to get started with building these relationships is to gather information from families before school starts. Consider sending a letter, email, or other communication home on or before the first day of school that includes information about your background and communicates your expectation that you intend to work with families and communities to support the student on their learning journey that year. This letter might be accompanied by an invitation to have families share knowledge about their child with you, either in writing, on the phone, or in person, so that a dialogue can begin. Parents love to brag about their children, and an invitation to do so by their child's teacher often can get a relationship off to a good start.

Alternatively, some teachers might opt to call, email, text, or speak in person with a few families each day, and after beginning with an "everything is fine" statement as reassurance, share a moment from the day having to do with their child that they saw as meaningful and would communicate their understanding of the child's strengths. Interactions such as these can build trust and open a space for conversations that might happen throughout the school year. Parents and caregivers are more likely to see a teacher as someone they can work with if they feel confident that the teacher also knows, appreciates, and is on the side of their child.

Reflection

- How do you connect with your students' families?
- Which of the things discussed in this section do you think you could incorporate into your practice?

When You Are with Them: What to Think about and Do during Your Time Together

Building relationships is the daily work of teachers. Whether it is teacher-student relationships, peer relationships, or relationships between students and the content being taught, schools need to cultivate and support social ties, develop ongoing participation, and provide opportunities to meaningfully contribute to the classroom and school community.

Teachers as Brain Scientists

Cozolino (2013) describes teachers as "neuroscientists attempting to use epigenetic processes to reshape the brains of students in ways that enhance their ability to think, learn, and act in more thoughtful and considerate ways" (p. 42). Teachers do this by working with students to build a classroom environment grounded in collective cohesion, community, and accountability. When this happens, students can feel connected and safe at school (Hammond, 2015), creating the potential to change their social and academic trajectories for the better. Practices such as inviting student voices and collaboration in the context of a set of shared values and expectations that include fairness and equity also are helpful (Ardell & Curwen, 2021). A teacher's positive affect, encouraging stance, and sense of humor, coupled with an inviting, engaging, and intellectually stimulating curriculum, also can help to make school welcoming. As a result, students begin to see themselves as capable and work toward a positive sense of self while learning that school is a safe place to ask questions, take risks, be vulnerable, and grow from mistakes.

Like Reggio Emilia schools, classrooms centered around positive relationships have certain characteristics (Cozolino, 2013). There is generally a low level of stress coupled with attentiveness to students' socioemotional needs. This combination can result in a sense of belonging and a feeling of self-efficacy that buffers students from the inevitabilities of adversity and helps them instead to cope, thrive, and look beyond themselves toward the community's needs. These classrooms help students to better learn about who they are and to be more open to academic learning as the parts of the brain work together.

Promising Practices

Many options are available for children to become limbically known by their teachers through particular pedagogical practices. As noted, it takes intentionality to make children feel welcome and valued in their classrooms. There are many ways to do this effectively, including through language, the curriculum, and the social environment.

Using Language Purposefully

The Responsive Classroom (www.responsiveclassroom.org) has multiple concrete strategies for teachers to use. One personal favorite is their thoughtfulness toward teachers' use of language (Denton, 2016). Through careful phrasing of their own talk, teachers can engage linguistic patterns that communicate ways to help students see themselves as capable (envisioning language) and to know that their effort matters (reinforcing language). Teachers also can engage in practices that enable students to become more independent and responsible (reminding language) and provide quick ways to get them refocused (redirecting language). Persistent open-ended questions also work to foster a sense of intellectual curiosity in students (Denton, 2016).

How teachers talk to students communicates how they see them. Purposeful use of language also suggests how students might come to see themselves and each other. Some examples of these language types include:

- "Let's remember how we thought like scientists yesterday, using evidence to confirm or refute our hypotheses, and use that skill again in today's work." (envisioning language)
- "Juan, you are using your best effort to solve a difficult math problem. That is perseverance in action." (reinforcing language)

- "Take a look at our classroom agreements. What can we do right now to make sure our classroom is a place where everyone can learn?" (reminding language)
- "Sarah, what do you need to be doing right now to get ready for recess?" (redirecting language)
- "What helped you to learn today?" (open-ended questioning)

Coupling careful use of language with an affect that communicates caring and concern helps students to read the situation and stay accountable. As Hammond (2015) notes, teachers who act as "warm demanders" (Kleinfeld, 1975) can obtain a balance of letting students know that they are valued while also having high expectations for their behavior and learning.

> **Being a Warm Demander**
>
> Truly knowing students can be your most powerful tool as a teacher. Many years ago, I (Amy) visited a middle school to observe a student teacher whom I was supervising. As I was walking across the campus during lunchtime, I spotted some of my former students from the elementary school where I had taught 4th and 5th grade. I went over to say hello and see how they were doing. It was a friendly reunion, and it was fun for me to see how they had grown and changed. The bell rang, and the students began heading back toward their classrooms. One of my former (and one of my all-time favorite) students threw his lunch trash into the bushes before heading off. I called him back and asked why he made that choice when the trash can was only a few steps away. He looked at me and tried to come up with an answer, but I could tell that even he could not explain it. I said, "Lawrence, I know you are going to go back into the bushes, retrieve the trash, and put it in the trash can before you go to your next class." He looked at me, took a deep breath, and asked me how I knew that. I replied, "Because I know the kind of person you are, and you are a person

> who cares for his community." He smiled and checked to see that no one was around to see him. He then went into the bushes, got the paper sack, put it into the trash can, and waved goodbye. Even after not having taught him for many years, I still knew Lawrence, and he had felt that, giving us both an opportunity to allow for a moment of "warm demanding" to work successfully.

Using Curriculum Purposefully

Teachers also must be conscious of their role in building relationships between students and academic content, and much has been written about the value of culturally responsive teaching practices (e.g., Gay, 2002; Ladson-Billings, 1994/2009). Because students interpret information through cultural lenses that come from their lived experiences, it becomes difficult to attune to the classroom environment when there is a substantial mismatch Hammond (2015). In addition, because students must pay attention if they are to learn, without a way to integrate new information or skills into existing funds of knowledge (Moll et al., 1992), they may find the classroom to be a confusing place. Sometimes teachers interpret this misunderstanding as indicating a need for less challenging work, but, in fact, the opposite is needed to expand students' synapses. Paying attention to students' cultural experiences and bringing them into conversation with the standards that teachers must teach becomes essential. Engaging in meaningful work, especially when it goes beyond the four walls of the classroom, helps students to have a sense of purpose (Curwen et al., 2019). Academic activities that are collaborative and dialogic encourage students to share various perspectives that help them to build meaningful ties as they learn together (Phillipson & Wegerif, 2017). Of course, it is important that teachers take a stance of presuming as little as possible about students' cultures, as a tendency to essentialize students' lived experiences based on stereotypes or assumptions can undo any good intentions.

Hammond (2015) asserts that teachers should acknowledge that students of color may have complex relationships with schools. Systemic racism, internalized oppression, ongoing microaggressions, and other factors can cause what she calls an "amygdala hijack." When this happens, it becomes overwhelmingly challenging to learn because the immediate threat response overrides everything else. Countering these feelings with affirmations (Ladson-Billings, 1994/2009) is necessary to create the conditions for students to thrive. Providing feedback in ways that are straightforward and productive also can be encouraging. Because doing so can look different for various learners, teachers might ask students to tell them what constructive criticism looks and sounds like to them. Hammond offers an asset-based feedback protocol. Teachers begin one-on-one conversations with students about their well-being before collaborating with them to identify strengths, needs, and specific ways to move their work toward excellence. Ending the meeting by having the student discuss what he or she heard as a reminder of your authentic belief in the student's ability to be successful helps to reinforce the idea that the feedback is not given to judge but, rather, to confirm a student's potential.

In the best of scenarios, schoolwork can help students to know their communities better, engendering a sense of pride through a sense of place. Using the funds of knowledge approach (Moll et al., 1992) mentioned earlier, teachers can engage community resources to support the curriculum. These connections might include going on a field trip to the public library, writing a letter to a city councilperson about an important local issue, or bringing in a guest speaker who can offer needed expertise. Similarly, teachers can draw curriculum from current community issues, helping to scaffold student participation as democratic citizens. For example, after a recent wildfire event, students in one special education elementary school classroom worked to raise funds to buy pet food for displaced dogs and cats temporarily housed in animal shelters. During this investigation, they sharpened their math, reading, writing, art, and social studies skills in the context of a project that amplified their talents in a way visible to the school community and beyond. In these and other scenarios, the hope is that students can expand their understanding of possibilities for the future while also feeling connected to their neighborhood, town, or city in the present.

Using the Social Environment Purposefully

A third key aspect of relationship building in the classroom is among the students themselves. As noted, schools are important sites for learning how to function in the social world. In a classroom microsystem, teachers effectively create the world in which their students live and learn each year. As we have argued, putting relationships at the center of the classroom experience is key. As Immordino-Yang (2016) states, motivation is "simultaneously cognitive and emotional, inherently embodied, and possessing both conscious and nonconscious dimensions" (p. 166). Therefore, considering all aspects of the classroom environment as they relate to the whole child has important implications for learning.

Multiple strategies can facilitate a sense of belonging that propels student learning. Practices that encourage storytelling and narratives to bond a community and create a sense of shared culture and values (Cozolino, 2013; Hammond, 2015) are a critical first step. Constructivist teaching practices engage learners in theory-making and problem-solving activities, thereby giving them space to develop their understandings with the support of the larger social environment. Having multiple ways for students to demonstrate what they know to their community through universal design for learning (Meyer et al., 2014) allows them to make choices and have a sense of agency. It also creates space for honoring multiple ways of knowing and helps students to see a place for themselves and their peers in the classroom's intellectual work. Opportunities to engage students' imaginations and creativity are essential, as they invite emotion and intuition to the learning endeavor (Immordino-Yang, 2016). Journaling to encourage students to reflect on their role in the world around them also is helpful (Cozolino, 2013; Immordino-Yang, 2016). In these ways, creating the social and academic environments happens simultaneously through instruction that is culturally responsive and relational in nature.

Creating familiar and consistent routines and rituals for interactions helps students to clarify how to be with one another in the classroom space. Discourse patterns, well-articulated classroom norms and values, and structured protocols also help them to understand the interconnections and interdependencies between them as a group of people. Within these structures, teachers can help students to shape the language they need to use with each other. For example, having students reflect on a conflict by asking them, "When you chose to call your friend a [silly name], what was your intention? Now that you can see how he [or she] reacted, what do you see as the impact of that choice?" shapes the learning community as a place where the process matters as much as the product. It also communicates that vulnerability as a learner matters more than perfection. In this way, having children identify the solutions that would work for them to resolve a conflict, rather than having consequences imposed by the teacher, can be powerful. As students learn to understand each other's social cues and their own triggers through a process of ongoing personal and collective reflection, the classroom becomes a place where relationships have the potential to grow and deepen in meaningful ways.

Because the social world can be challenging, working in solidarity with students to build community and work through conflict is vital. Circle processes and restorative justice practices (e.g., Pranis, 2015; Zehr, 2015) can be helpful tools. As Amstutz and Mullet (2015) note, a restorative approach to conflict resolution engages the community in collaborative problem solving that offers a mechanism for accountability, responsibility, and personal reflection. These dialogues consider the specific incident, that is, the relationship of the harmer to both the directly harmed and the larger community, and are undergirded by a desire to repair relationships. Attention is also paid to any role the existing social system might have played, offering opportunities to go beyond resolving interpersonal issues alone and incorporating possibilities for systemic transformation. Given that emotions are closely tied to learning (Immordino-Yang, 2016), this work is not separate from academic tasks but, rather, supports them.

Human relationships are constantly under construction and need ongoing attention for them to work well. Through a deliberate centering of positive relationships, teachers and students can learn and grow together in the context of a microsystem that makes its members feel valued and valuable to the classroom community. When teachers extend this work to actors in students' mesosystems, they create a partnership of complementary support and care that often translates to stronger student connections, socially and intellectually. In the next chapter, we move beyond this fundamental work into recognizing when students need their teachers to respond to mental health concerns.

Takeaways

- Our brains, especially the limbic system, have evolved to connect socially.
- Limbic resonance and limbic revision are processes that enable deep connections to change and repair the brain.
- Building relationships is key to academic learning and positive mental health.
- Building relationships should be done with intention and planning.
- We can use language, the curriculum, and the overall social environment to enhance relationships.

Note

1. One resource is an online course, *Neuroscience & the Classroom: Making Connections.* Provided by the Annenberg Foundation in collaboration with researchers from Harvard and the University of Southern California, it can be found on the Annenberg Learner website: https://www.learner.org/series/neuroscience-in-the-classroom/.

References

Amstutz, L. S., & Mullet, J. H. (2015). *The little book of restorative discipline for schools: Teaching responsibility; Creating caring climates*. Skyhorse.

Ardell, A. L., & Curwen, M. S. (2021). "Multiple perspectives and many connections": Systems thinking and student voice. In L. Hogg, K. Stockbridge, C. Achieng-Everson, & S. SooHoo (Eds.), *Pedagogies of with-ness: Students, teachers, voice and agency* (pp. 117–128). Meyers Education Press.

Arvidson, J., Kinniburgh, K., Howard, K., Spinazzola, J., Strothers, H., Evans, M., Andres, B., Cohen, C., & Blaustein, M. E. (2011). Treatment of complex trauma in young children: Developmental and cultural considerations in application of the ARC intervention model. *Journal of Child & Adolescent Trauma, 4*, 34–51.

Bronfenbrenner, U. (1979). *The ecology of human development: Experiments by nature and design*. Harvard University Press.

Cozolino, L. (2013). *The social neuroscience of education: Optimizing attachment and learning in the classroom*. W. W. Norton and Company.

Curwen, M., Ardell, A., & MacGillivray, L. (2019). Hopeful discourse: Elementary children's activist responses to modern-day slavery grounded in systems thinking. *Literacy Research: Theory, Methods, and Practice, 68*, 139–161.

Davis, B., Sumara, D., & Luce-Kapler, R. (2015). *Engaging minds: Cultures of education and practices of teaching* (3rd ed.). Routledge.

Denton, P. (2016). *The power of our words for middle school: Teacher language that helps students learn*. Center for Responsive Schools, Inc.

Edwards, C., Gandini, L., & Forman, G. (1998). *The hundred languages of children: The Reggio Emilia approach—Advanced reflections* (2nd ed.). ABC-CLIO.

Fredricks, J. A., Blumenfeld, P. C., & Paris, A. H. (2004). School engagement: Potential of the concept, state of the evidence. *Review of Educational Research, 74*(1), 59–109.

Gay, G. (2002). Preparing for culturally responsive teaching. *Journal of Teacher Education, 53*(2), 106–116.

Hammond, Z. (2015). *Culturally responsive teaching and the brain: Promoting authentic engagement and rigor among culturally and linguistically diverse students*. Corwin.

Immordino-Yang, M. H. (2016). *Emotions, learning, and the brain: Exploring the educational implications of affective neuroscience*. W. W. Norton and Company.

Kleinfeld, J. (1975). Effective teachers of Eskimo and Indian students. *School Review*, *83*(2), 301–344.

Ladson-Billings, G. (1994/2009). *The dreamkeepers: Successful teachers of African-American children*. Jossey-Bass.

Lewis, T., Amini, F., & Lannon, R. (2001). *A general theory of love*. Knopf Doubleday.

Masten, A. S. (2014). *Ordinary magic: Resilience in development*. The Guilford Press.

Meyer, A., Rose, D. H., & Gordon, D. (2014). *Universal design for learning: Theory and practice*. CAST Professional.

Moll, L. C., Amanti, C., Neff, D., & Gonzalez, N. (1992). Funds of knowledge for teaching: Using a qualitative approach to connect homes and classrooms. *Theory into Practice*, *31*(2), 132–141.

Phillipson, N., & Wegerif, R. (2017). *Dialogic education: Mastering core concepts through thinking together*. Routledge.

Pranis, K. (2015). *The little book of circle processes: A new/old approach to peacemaking*. Skyhorse.

Zehr, H. (2015). *The little book of restorative justice* (2nd ed.). Skyhorse.

4

Recognizing Students' Mental Health Problems

In addition to promoting healthy relationships in their classrooms, teachers are often the first adults to notice the signs of mental health problems. Thus, they play an essential role in the process of connecting children to needed supports and treatment. In Chapter 2, we referred to this role as a "gateway provider" (Stiffman et al., 2010). The assumption behind a gateway provider is that children and youth need the assistance of a knowledgeable adult to access services. This support must start with recognition of need but, later in the process, also can take the form of advice, encouragement, and guidance about the next steps (Stiffman et al., 2001). Although teachers are not the only people in children's lives who can function as gateway providers, they have the advantage of daily contact with students and frequent opportunities to observe how children respond to academic and social demands. Thus, teachers are critically important in ensuring that students receive the care they need.

The importance of improving teachers' ability to recognize and respond to students' mental health problems is highlighted by the consistent finding that few of the children identified as needing mental health services receive them. For example, several studies have shown that the percentage of children with a diagnosis of a mental health disorder who receive services ranges from only 20% to 40% (Adelman & Taylor, 2012; Kessler

DOI: 10.4324/9780367810269-4

et al., 2001; Strein et al., 2003). It is also noteworthy that most of the students who receive services access them at school (Burns et al., 1995; Wiley & Cory, 2013). Kaplan et al. (1998) found that adolescents were ten times more likely to access mental health services if they had access to school-based mental health services than were students without access to such services. Research on students' use of school-based mental health services has shown improvements in mental health symptoms, school attendance, and grades (Ballard et al., 2014).

To accomplish our goal of helping teachers to be more effective gateway providers, in this chapter, we provide more detail about the prevalence of mental health problems, discuss how these problems typically express themselves, and provide a framework and rubric to guide teachers toward recognition of mental health issues. In subsequent chapters, we build on this information with specific information on how to facilitate identification and referral for services.

A Framework for Understanding Mental Health Problems

As we discussed in Chapter 1, data gathered over at least 25 years suggest that a surprisingly number of students have mental health problems (e.g., Adelman & Taylor, 2012; Burns et al., 1995). These studies have varied in their methodology and, thus, offer different estimates of overall prevalence. Nevertheless, a consensus of around 20% in a 12-month period has emerged. Estimates of lifetime prevalence, as opposed to a 12-month period, are even higher. For example, a study of over 10,000 adolescents from 12 to 18 years old found that nearly half of those in the study suffered from a diagnosable mental health disorder by the time that they reached late adolescence (Ries Merikangas et al., 2009). The same study found that the chances of having more than one disorder also were high; about one in four of those who had one disorder were affected by a second disorder.

It is important to note that these data are typically based on the formal diagnostic categories found in the *Diagnostic and Statistical Manual* (American Psychiatric Association, 2013). As we discussed in Chapter 2, there are many problems with classifying children using formal categories, including reliability and treatment validity. In addition, a significant number of children meet the criteria for diagnosis with a mental health disorder but do not suffer significant impairment, as suggested by the research on the dual-factor model of mental health. At the same time, many children do not meet the formal criteria for a disorder but still suffer significant challenges in coping with school and life.

Although we have discussed mental health problems in the context of formal diagnoses, in part because this is how much of the data are organized, we also understand that knowledge of formal diagnoses, per se, does not necessarily help teachers to recognize mental health problems in their students or make them effective gateway providers. Categorical labels, such as those used by the *Diagnostic and Statistical Manual* (American Psychiatric Association, 2013), provide limited information about how to help children with mental health problems and run the risk of creating an illusion of knowledge. For example, we have heard many educators, including teachers, administrators, counselors, and school psychologists, say something such as, "Oh, he has ADHD [attention deficit hyperactivity disorder], so that is the way he behaves." The problem with such a statement is that it can foreclose curiosity about the needs of individual children, who are, of course, more than their labels.

Another, more practical, way of understanding mental health problems comes from analyses of how problem behaviors and symptoms cluster together and are expressed (Caspi et al., 2014). Several studies have shown that problem behaviors and symptoms can be empirically classified into three broad dimensions: internalizing problems, externalizing problems, and thought disorders (Kotov et al., 2011).

Internalizing problems include sadness, loss of motivation or withdrawal from activities that were once enjoyed, excessive worrying, social withdrawal, and physical problems in the absence of a known physical illness, including headaches, stomachaches, and other physical complaints that we associate with excessive stress or tension (Whitcomb & Merrell, 2013). These symptoms are forms of subjective distress and suffering that are not necessarily obvious to an outside observer. The most common expressions of internalizing problems are depression and anxiety.

Externalizing problems include aggression, impulsivity and overactivity, defiance or opposition to authority, and violation of social norms, such as lying, stealing, and bullying (Farmer et al., 2009; Whitcomb & Merrell, 2013). These behaviors are usually apparent to an outside observer. Children with externalizing problems include those who have attention deficit hyperactivity disorder (ADHD), oppositional defiant disorder (ODD), or conduct disorder.

Although most research supports these two primary dimensions of behavior, researchers have also suggested that thought disorders may constitute a third dimension (Kotov et al., 2011). Thought disorders include behavior such as confused or disorganized thinking, delusions, and hallucinations (American Psychiatric Association, 2013). An adolescent who develops schizophrenia and begins to hear voices would be an example of someone who has a thought disorder. When the data from large groups of children and adolescents are analyzed, however, these three dimensions emerge as mainly distinct, and it is important to remember that, in individual children, these kinds of problems can co-occur. For example, it is not unusual for someone with ADHD to also struggle with anxiety.

To illustrate these three dimensions, consider the following four scenarios:

Scenario 1

Alicia is a 16-year-old girl who is frequently tardy for her early periods and is often absent for vague reasons, such as "not feeling well" or "headaches." She is quiet and well behaved in her classes but rarely raises her hand to answer questions or participate in whole-class discussions. Alicia also never asks for help from the teacher, although, in some classes, such as math and English, she does not seem to understand assignments. She also reports being fearful of doing class presentations. Alicia has Ds in most of her classes and an F in physical education because she avoids undressing. When her English teacher looked at her cumulative record, it appeared that her grades began to drop in middle school. Later, when her English teacher casually asks her what she is going to do during an upcoming weekend, she mentions going out to eat with her family and hanging out with her siblings. When the teacher asks, "Oh, do you see any of your friends?" Alicia responds that she doesn't see anybody other than family members outside of school. Alicia also mentions that she was severely bullied as a sophomore, which led to an increase in her headaches.

Alicia is someone who has significant internalizing problems. Her frequent headaches and vague complaints of not feeling well, frequent tardiness, withdrawal, and shyness, along with her poor grades, suggest she is likely experiencing a great deal of anxiety. Although it appears that anxiety significantly impairs her ability to function in school, as seen in poor grades, absences, limited participation, and self-advocacy, Alicia's problems may not stand out in the classroom because she is well behaved. It also might be easy to explain her problems away by saying that her "moodiness" is typical of adolescent girls, a stereotype at best. Although less likely to be noticed by her teachers, over time, she will become increasingly at risk for serious problems, such as dropping out of school or failing to graduate on time.

Scenario 2

Aaron is a 15-year-old high school transgender student who had been hospitalized for threatening to commit suicide. When he came back to school, he enrolled in only four classes because it was difficult for him to last an entire day at school. Aaron reported that he felt too overwhelmed when he tried to make it through a full school day. In class, Aaron seems irritable and cranky. He snaps at his neighbors

> in class and doesn't seem to socialize with other students. Aaron finishes most of his classwork but doesn't complete much homework. When his health teacher discussed this with him, he said that, when he comes home from school, he usually goes to bed and sleeps until dinner. Soon after dinner, he goes to bed and again sleeps until morning. Aaron tells his health teacher that he used to enjoy hanging out with friends and playing soccer but no longer enjoys those things and "doesn't see the point." He is currently earning a D, two Fs, and one C in his four classes.

Aaron (Scenario 2) is also someone with significant internalizing problems, although they manifest differently than do those of Alicia. While Alicia appears to be experiencing a high level of anxiety, Aaron's internalizing difficulties look more like depression. His hospitalization for threatening suicide is, of course, worrisome, but so is his chronic irritability, lack of energy, oversleeping, and loss of interest in things he used to enjoy. We typically view sadness as a primary expression of depression, but a loss of motivation or enjoyment of activities once found pleasurable is an essential symptom. The technical term for this is *anhedonia*. It is also not unusual in children and adolescents for sadness to be accompanied by frequent irritability (American Psychiatric Association, 2013).

Often, transgender students, such as Aaron, are grouped with other sexual minority populations, yet there is a growing recognition that transgender youth have needs unique from lesbian, gay, bisexual, transgender, and questioning or queer youth (LGBTQ+) students. The results of the National School Climate Survey found that transgender youth experience harassment and assault more frequently than do non-transgender youth (Greytak et al., 2009). Specifically, transgender youth are frequently exposed to defamatory, derogatory, or biased language at school from their peers and sometimes even from teachers or staff members (Gay, Lesbian and Straight Education Network, 2014; Greytak et al., 2009). These experiences put transgender youth at higher risk for mental health problems while in school and later in life (Greytak et al., 2009).

Scenario 3

Ken is an almost 7-year-old first grade student. His teacher thinks that he is smart and "gets" new concepts quickly. He is pleasant when he is participating in activities that he enjoys, such as playing card games or soccer on the playground. Yet, Ken has trouble sustaining attention to class assignments and seems to overreact when he must participate in an activity that he does not like. When he does not get what he wants, he cries loudly and will sometimes be physically aggressive with other students by hitting or pushing them. Ken seems to have the most difficulty when he has to transition from one activity to another. These problems occur daily.

Ken (Scenario 3) fits the profile of a student who exhibits several externalizing problems. These include verbal and physical aggression, impulsivity (overreacting when he must participate in an activity that he does not like), and difficulty paying attention. Given Ken's age, some teachers might think that Ken is simply immature. It is important to understand that it is rare for children to outgrow behaviors such as Ken's. Instead, without intervention, these behaviors are likely to grow more severe over time.

Scenario 4

Quan is a 17-year-old senior in high school. For his first three years of high school, he earned mostly earned As and Bs in his classes. Late last semester, Quan missed almost a month of school. It was rumored that he had been in the hospital, but the reasons for this are not clear. Although Quan had always been shy, when he returned to school, he rarely spoke to his peers in class or to his teachers. He also started to wear a jacket or hoodie in class, even when the weather was warm. Quan's writing, which had seemed adequate before, became rambling and tended

> toward off-topic rants. His history teacher approached him one day to check in with him and find out whether he was okay. Quan seemed nervous and did not make eye contact. He became agitated as he complained about his parents' using drugs at home (the history teacher knew the parents and thought that this was very unlikely). After a few moments, he abruptly ended the conversation and walked out of the classroom.

Quan is an example of someone who might be developing a thought disorder. We say "might" because there are also possible physical causes or, in some cases, traumatic events that might trigger at least some of these symptoms. Nevertheless, we imagine that teachers would find Quan's behaviors troubling or even alarming and would quickly seek help from a mental health professional on campus.

Each of these scenarios in different ways represents serious problems, yet research suggests that teachers are more likely to be concerned about and refer children with externalizing problems (Loades & Mastroyannopoulou, 2010; Splett et al., 2019). This bias toward externalizing problems has been called the "squeaky wheel" phenomenon (Bradshaw et al., 2008; Splett et al., 2019). In this case, the squeaky wheel is the child who causes problems for the teacher because they (or he; they are often male) disrupts class and interrupts learning for others.

Nevertheless, teachers recognize the need to identify children, such as Alicia and Aaron, who have internalizing problems but feel they do not have the training to do so effectively (Papandrea & Winefield, 2011; Rothì et al., 2008). The challenge for teachers to identify and refer children with internalizing problems is apparent in research findings that show that teachers can identify only about half the children in their classrooms with elevated levels of depression and anxiety, the primary expressions of internalizing problems (Cunningham & Suldo, 2014).

Although this bias toward the squeaky wheel is understandable, it can, unfortunately, lead to the neglect of students with less obvious internalizing symptoms, such as anxiety or depression. Correcting this is critical because internalizing problems, such as anxiety, depression, social withdrawal, and loss of motivation, are common, long-lasting, and pose significant challenges to being successful in school and life. As stated above, teachers recognize these problems as serious in the abstract but struggle to recognize them in their students. To assist teachers in recognizing internalizing problems, we further explore their most common expressions: anxiety and depression.

Anxiety is characterized by excessive worry or fears or both (American Psychiatric Association, 2013). It is also common for children with excessive worry or fear to have physical complaints, such as muscle tension, headaches, or stomachaches. Anxiety disorders are some of the most common mental health problems seen in children and adolescents (Rapee et al., 2009). In a given calendar year, between 5% and 6% of children or adolescents have a diagnosable anxiety disorder (Burns et al., 1995; Costello et al., 2003; Ghandour et al., 2019). By the time that students graduate high school, between one-quarter and one-third of the population will have experienced an anxiety disorder (Copeland et al., 2014; Kessler et al., 2009). Rates of anxiety disorders rise during adolescence but, surprisingly and potentially pointing to a gender bias in how we view anxiety, there is not convincing evidence for a substantial difference between males and females (Ghandour et al., 2019).

Like Alicia in Scenario 1, students with anxiety disorders experience significant academic difficulties (Muroff & Ross, 2011; Mychailyszyn et al., 2010). One study that examined these academic challenges found that the most common academic problems among students with elevated levels of anxiety related to concentrating on work and giving oral reports or reading aloud (Nail et al., 2015). Remember that Alicia did not seem to understand her assignments in several of her classes. Not understanding could easily be the result of difficulty concentrating on classroom instructions. Her difficulty in understanding her assignments is also compounded by not asking for help or participating in class discussions, which removes her from other opportunities to learn about her assignments. As we noted above, Alicia is also afraid of making oral presentations in front of the class. This is akin to her difficulties with asking for help or participating, as these activities, like oral presentations, require exposure to others with all of the feelings of vulnerability that they can elicit in anxious students.

Symptoms of anxiety often co-occur with depression, but depression has its own unique characteristics. Depression's primary expression in children or adolescents involves chronic sadness or irritability and loss of energy or motivation (American Psychiatric Association, 2013). It is estimated that about 6% of youth over a 12-month period have a depressive disorder (American Academy of Pediatrics, Committee on School Health, 2004; Costello et al., 2006) with a lifetime rate of about 14% (Merikangas et al., 2010). Unlike anxiety, these rates are nearly double for adolescents as compared to younger children (Ghandour et al., 2019).

Before adolescence, there is not a significant difference between young boys and girls in how often depression occurs; however, rates of depression are much higher for adolescent females than for males (Costello et al., 2006; Ghandour et al., 2019). This suggests that a significant amount of the increase of depression in adolescence is accounted for by females. Although less common than anxiety, the long-term consequences of depression are serious. Due to loss of productivity and a lower quality of life associated with depression, the World Health Organization estimates that, by 2030, depression will be the leading cause of disability in the world (Yang et al., 2015). Depression is also often associated with suicide (Stewart et al., 2016).

Like anxiety, depression can have an adverse impact on a student's success in school and later in life. In Aaron's scenario, several symptoms seem to interfere with his being successful in school. These include his frequent irritability, apparent fatigue, and loss of motivation. Although chronic irritability certainly makes it more difficult for Aaron to connect with his teachers and peers, it is the loss of motivation and the accompanying lack of energy that will hinder him the most from attending a full day of school, finishing his homework, earning enough credits to graduate, or connecting with friends or supportive adults. This loss of motivation, or anhedonia, is the most impairing symptom of depression, resulting in more frequent, longer-lasting, and more severe episodes (Gabbay et al., 2015).

> **Reflection**
> - What has been your experience with children with internalizing problems, such as anxiety or depression?
> - What signs did you see that let you know that those students were distressed?

Teachers are much more likely to refer males than females for mental health concerns (Loades & Mastroyannopoulou, 2010). In addition, as they grow older, males diagnosed with mental health disorders are perceived as being more impaired than are females who are diagnosed (Costello et al., 2003). The discrepancy is, in part, accounted for by the finding that males are much more likely to be diagnosed with externalizing problems than are females.

Two of the most common types of externalizing problems are ADHD and ODD. For both diagnoses, boys far outnumber girls. For example, in studies that consider samples of the general population, three times as many boys are diagnosed with ADHD as compared to girls (Barkley, 2006). When this is narrowed down to those who are referred for professional help for ADHD, the ratio of boys to girls rises dramatically to up to nine to one (Bruchmüller et al., 2012). Boys are also about two times more likely to be diagnosed with ODD, which frequently co-occurs with ADHD.

Although it is possible that more boys than girls have externalizing problems, such as ADHD or ODD, it is also possible that gender bias plays a role in the disparity. For example, when presented with vignettes that describe boys and girls with symptoms of ADHD, therapists were much more likely to diagnosis boys with ADHD, even when the symptoms described were the same as those of girls (Bruchmüller et al., 2012). In the same study, in the vignettes about males, the males were more likely to be diagnosed with ADHD, even if they did not meet the formal criteria for such a diagnosis.

Data from several studies suggest that culture, as understood as ethnic or racial identification (e.g., Latinx, Vietnamese

American, African American), does not have a strong influence on the likelihood of having a mental health problem (Brown, 2012; Burns et al., 1995; Costello et al., 1996; Rutter, 2003). Yet, there are significant cultural differences in whom teachers refer for mental health services. A notable example is African American males. African American students, especially boys, are more likely to be referred for services than are White, Latinx, or Asian American students (Vazquez & Villodas, 2019). These differences remain even after accounting for differences in family structures, income, and academic functioning. In addition, African American students are nearly twice as likely to be given a label of an emotional/behavioral disorder than are White students (Harvard Civil Rights Project, 2000) and much more likely to be suspended or expelled (Cokley et al., 2015). This pattern of suspensions and expulsions begins as early as preschool.

At least some of these disparities appear to be accounted for by the perceived presence of externalizing problems in African American children (Vazquez & Villodas, 2019). In other words, teachers are more likely to perceive African American children as being defiant and aggressive. Because teachers are more likely to refer students due to externalizing problems, more African American students are referred. There is considerable evidence that this bias arises from how African American students are perceived and treated.

For example, teachers are more likely to expect African American students to misbehave than they expect of White students (Kunesh & Noltemeyer, 2019). Teachers also are more likely to perceive African American students' behaviors as angry and aggressive when their parents do not (Munzer et al., 2018), suggesting a significant cultural gap. In another study, pre-service teachers read a vignette about an ambiguously defiant student. Those who read vignettes about an African American student believed that the student was more likely than was a White student to misbehave in the future (Kunesh & Noltemeyer, 2019). The authors argue that perceiving defiance as a stable trait, less amiable to change than behaviors that arise from circumstances, leaves teachers feeling less competent to intervene and, thus, less motivated to act.

It is noteworthy that these studies do not suggest explicit bias but rather implicit, mainly unconscious, biases. Although not explicit, they still result in multiple problems, including less supportive relationships between teachers and students and loss of instructional time. These, in turn, lead to further problems, such as more acting out, office referrals, suspensions, and expulsions.

There are multiple problems with these biases, but from a mental health perspective, there are two that are particularly important to consider. One is that African American students can be referred when mental health treatment is not needed. If the problem can be solved or at least significantly improved by a stronger student-teacher relationship, better home-school communication, or more academic support, mental health treatment becomes an expensive, intrusive, and ultimately ineffective intervention. The other concern, which brings us back to our discussion of externalizing and internalizing problems, is that teachers' interpretation of the behavior of African American students, often boys, as being impulsive, oppositional, or aggressive may limit their ability to identify underlying internalizing problems (Cokley et al., 2015). This is a problem that African American males share with other male students, but for these students, the intersection of gender and race appears to exasperate the issue.

Although challenging for teachers, the identification of children with internalizing and externalizing problems is critical for effective prevention of long-term mental health and educational problems. In the next section, we discuss how teachers can think about students in their classrooms and present a rubric that will facilitate identification and make referrals to other resources easier.

Recognizing the Signs of a Mental Health Problem: Typical or Troubled

Before we explain the process of recognizing children who might need mental health treatment or other social and emotional support, it is essential to point out that we are not asking teachers to diagnose students or even to say definitively that a child or adolescent needs mental health treatment. It would be professionally inappropriate and potentially harmful for teachers to do so. Instead, we present the externalizing/internalizing/thought disorder framework as a way for teachers to understand how mental health problems are expressed.

With this understanding, teachers still play an essential role in an initial screening and referral process. Some of those students who are "screened in" for further consideration for mental health supports by teachers will, in the end, not need mental health treatment. Others clearly will. Because teachers are "front line," they are situated at the beginning of this decision-making process. The expectation is that teachers should be knowledgeable about mental health problems and actively engaged in the process of identifying students who might need help. At this initial stage, however, they are not required to be 100% certain about their judgments.

Questions to Assist with the Recognition of Mental Health Problems

What we aspire to in this section is to present a kind of "thinking tool" or rubric. In this sense, the six questions below are designed to help teachers organize their thinking about a student and decide whether further action is necessary.

1. What, specifically, is the student doing or not doing that troubles you?
2. How have these behaviors had an impact on the student's learning? How do you think these behaviors affect the student socially?
3. Do these behaviors seem typical or atypical?
   a. Are these behaviors developmentally appropriate?
   b. What would the consequences of these behaviors be later in the child's development?
   c. How intense are these problems?
      i. How long?
      ii. How frequent?
      iii. Rate on a scale of 1 to 10.

4. What do you think the student is feeling? What do you think the student is thinking about your class, school, and his or her life in general?
5. What is going on in a student's life that might contribute to these behaviors?
6. Who is this student connected to in a supportive way?

Questions 1 and 2 ask teachers to clarify their concerns to arrive at a more detailed picture of what behaviors are worrisome and how these seem to be affecting students' lives. Question 3 helps teachers to think through whether worrisome behaviors are bothersome, but typical, expressions of a child's development or represent something atypical and more troubling. The last three questions round out teachers' understanding of students' broader social context. Question 4 asks teachers to better understand the child's perspective on what is happening, and Questions 5 and 6 broaden teachers' perspectives by taking adversity and social support into consideration.

These questions serve multiple purposes. One purpose is to mitigate some of the biases that we discussed above. Despite our best efforts, our biases affect how we view children and whether we decide that they need help with mental health problems or not. These biases arise from a complex mix of our cultural and socioeconomic backgrounds, the unique circumstances of our families, and our unique experiences as individuals, including our training as educators. The challenge is that these biases about others often arise reflexively with little conscious effort.

Daniel Kahneman, a Nobel Award-winning economist, describes these automatic judgments or biases as one of two kinds of thinking that we employ to solve problems and make decisions (Kahneman, 2011). He calls these System 1 and System 2 thinking. System 1 functions quickly and automatically with little conscious effort, while System 2 involves focus and conscious effort. Kahneman states that, although System 1 thinking is generally accurate and efficient, it is prone to systematic biases or errors of judgment. Although not a perfect solution, in situations where bias is more likely to happen, more focus and effortful reflection from System 2 can reduce some of our automatic biases. As Kahneman explains, "The way to block errors that originate in System 1 is simple in principle; recognize the signs that you are in a cognitive minefield, slow down, and ask for reinforcement from System 2" (p. 417).

Reinforcement from System 2 can take the form of checklists or a series of questions, such as the one above. This strategy is supported by evidence that suggests that structured questionnaires help frame teachers' perceptions in ways that increase the accuracy of the identification of students who need support (Dowdy et al., 2013). Reinforcement also can take the form of information that leads us to recognize situations for which we need to slow down and consider our decisions more carefully.

> **Reflection**
>
> - Can you identify a time when biases about gender, race, or ethnicity may have influenced how you perceived a student's behavior?
> - What actions did you take or not take that was the result of that bias?

Another purpose is to make teachers more effective at communicating their concerns to other professionals. The more clear, detailed, and thoughtful our thinking is about why we believe children have mental health challenges and need additional support, the better we can advocate for their needs. In a sense, teachers need to become "bilingual" and express their concerns in a language to which mental health professionals are more likely to be receptive. Below, we discuss these concerns in more depth.

1. *What, specifically, is the student doing or not doing that troubles you?* Sometimes, students are doing several things, all of which seem alarming. If so, it is helpful to clarify your thinking by identifying the top three to five concerns you have. It is important to be as specific as possible. For

example, below are a teacher's top concerns about Alicia and, hypothetically, some of the underlying thoughts that led to their selection.

   a. She misses too much school because she is sick.
   "I wonder if something is seriously wrong physically. If not, what is going on? Either way, missing so much school is really affecting her grades."
   b. She rarely participates verbally in class or asks for help.
   "Okay, I have a few shy kids, but she really never says anything. The thing is, I know she doesn't always understand what we are doing and really needs to learn how to ask for help."
   c. She is currently earning Ds or Fs in all of her classes.
   "Despite everything, she is a nice kid. I know that she can do better than this. Yet, if this keeps up, she is not going to graduate, or she might have to transfer to an alternative education school."

Exercise

Reread Ken, Aaron, or Quan's scenario and list three to five behaviors that you think are priorities. For each priority behavior, write a brief note regarding why you think these behaviors are a priority.

2. *Do these behaviors seem typical or atypical?* Once these top concerns are clarified, the next step is to consider whether they are typical or atypical. In other words, regarding these behaviors that might be troublesome, are they typical aspects of development, and will they lessen with minimal intervention? Atypical behaviors seem unusual and are not likely to improve on their own. There are three aspects of this question to consider:

   a. The first is, *Are these behaviors developmentally appropriate?* When considering developmental expectations, it is crucial to separate developmental myths or stereotypes from what we know about development.

For example, occasional tantrums are not unusual for a 2- or 3-year-old child, but it is a myth that typical toddlers frequently throw a tantrum (although it may feel that way for the parent of a toddler). It is also developmentally appropriate for an adolescent to question adult authority. Still, it would be a stereotype to say that it is typical for teenagers to argue with their parents daily for weeks at a time.

For example, Alicia's behaviors are not merely the behaviors of a moody adolescent and do not seem developmentally appropriate. Teenagers can be moody, and a shyer student can participate less, but frequent absences for vaguely identified physical problems and never participating in class or asking for help are not developmentally typical. It is also noteworthy that Alicia does not socialize outside of school other than participating in activities with her family.

    b. Another way to look at these behaviors in developmental context is to consider, *What would the consequences of these behaviors be later in the child's development?* (Achenbach & Edelbrock, 1984). In considering this question, remember that, without support, students with social and emotional problems do not usually outgrow them on their own.

Again, using Alicia as an example, if a year passed and Alicia continued to miss classes and not participate, what would be the outcome? Possible outcomes include having to move to an alternative program to make up credits or even dropping out of school. It also seems quite possible that she would become increasingly isolated in her community. Whatever the specific outcome at school or home, without intervention and additional supports, Alicia's ability to be successful in school and life would be significantly disrupted. Her current challenges are likely to become more impairing in the future than they are now.

    c. The next question to ask, when deciding whether a student's behaviors are typical or atypical, is, *How intense are these problems?* Behaviors might be considered more intense if they occur frequently or have been going on for an extended time. Alicia's difficulties with anxiety seem to go back to middle school. This means that she has struggled with anxiety for at least three years, a long period of time by any standard. In addition, Alicia's challenges might not be considered serious if she had an off day once a month, but her difficulties with anxiety appear to be present every day.

Another straightforward way to clarify one's thinking about intensity is to use a metric, such as a 1 to 10 scale, like the scale used to rate pain in medical settings. At the low end of the scale, 1 would indicate that the behaviors in question are not a problem at all (you probably would not be thinking about this student), and at the high end of the scale, a 10 would be an extreme problem that requires immediate action. Alicia's situation might be rated a 7 or 8. She is not necessarily in an acute crisis, which we might rate a 9 or 10. At the same time, her problems with anxiety are chronic and require prompt and effective support to improve her functioning at school.

> **Exercise**
>
> Rate the intensity or severity of Ken's behaviors. Make a brief note regarding your reasoning.

3. Related to intensity are the questions: *How have these behaviors affected the student's learning? How have these behaviors affected the student socially?* Again, be as specific as possible. Take the top concerns for Alicia listed above:

   a. She misses too much school because she is sick.
   b. She rarely participates verbally in class or asks for help.
   c. She is currently earning Ds or Fs in all of her classes.

Missing school means that Alicia is also missing instruction and opportunities to solidify learning through discussion. She also is not completing in-class assignments, which reduces the time she has to practice or apply knowledge or skills learned. Not participating in class also takes away an essential aspect of learning.

Missing class and not participating when present also limits Alicia's social interactions and her ability to be "known" by her teachers and her peers

> **Exercise**
>
> Consider Aaron and answer these questions:
>
> 1. How have these behaviors affected the student's learning?
> 2. How have these behaviors affected the student socially?

4. The next set of questions can help teachers to better understand what a student is feeling or thinking. Understanding this is especially important for students who might have internalizing problems, such as anxiety or depression. *What do you think the student is feeling? What do you think the student is thinking about your class, school, and his or her life in general?* For example, you might reasonably imagine that Alicia is feeling anxious at times, even fearful. You also might imagine she worries about her grades and her future.

> **Exercise**
>
> What do you think Quan might be thinking or feeling?

5. The next question to ask is, *What is going on in a student's life that might contribute to these behaviors?* We know from our discussion of ACEs in Chapter 2 that adverse childhood experiences have long-lasting, negative effects. We expect teachers to investigate these issues, but we also recognize that teachers might know what stresses students are experiencing in their lives. Teachers are legally and ethically obligated to report specific adverse experiences, such as physical or emotional abuse or neglect, to the appropriate community agencies. Yet, many other stresses can adversely

affect children's lives. For example, a painful divorce or parents who are ill or suddenly unemployed can all cause a great deal of stress. These kinds of stresses might not have a significant impact on some students because they have the kinds of social and psychological resources that we associate with resilience. For other, more vulnerable students, stresses such as these might overwhelm their ability to cope effectively and lead them to manifest the kinds of challenges that we have discussed.

Alicia reports being severely bullied as a sophomore. There are two possibilities. One is that the bullying was stressful enough that it caused her anxiety. The second possibility is that she was anxious before the bullying, and this exacerbated a pre-existing condition. For our purposes, as teachers concerned about Alicia, this does not make a practical difference. In either case, it will be necessary for Alicia to reduce her physical tension and learn to feel safe at school. At the same time, this information might be useful in determining what kinds of supports or treatments Alicia needs later.

6. The last question asks us to shift our focus away from the symptoms and problems we have discussed up to this point and consider what sources of resilience a student might have. As we discussed in Chapter 2, critical to resilience is close relationships. Given this, it is important to ask, *Who is this student connected to in a supportive way?* Although Alicia does not seem to interact with many of her peers, she seems comfortable with spending time with her family. In addition, although we do not have all the details, her English teacher, who has gone out of her way to speak with her and look at her cumulative record, might be a supportive person in Alicia's life.

Summary: Why Would We Refer Alicia?

As we have considered Alicia's situation, we have identified specific behaviors that concern us and clarified how these behaviors might interfere with her ability to be successful in school. We have also considered whether Alicia's behavior and challenges at school are atypical rather than typical expressions of adolescent behavior. We have identified past stresses and potential social supports. This information prepares teachers to provide a well-thought-out rationale for seeking help for Alicia. For example, given our thinking about Alicia, a written statement, which is often required for a referral, might say:

> Alicia is a junior in my class. She is earning Ds and Fs in all of her classes. She often misses school because she is sick and rarely participates in class or asks for help.
>
> These things happen nearly every day, and, in looking at her records, I notice that this has been happening since middle school. I think that Alicia is much more anxious and fearful than usual and am worried that, if this goes on, she will have to move to an alternative program or even drop out of school. Alicia has told me she was severely bullied as a sophomore. She and I get along very well, and she seems to have a good relationship with her family. I look forward to talking more about how we can best help Alicia be more successful.

This statement accomplishes two things. One is that, in a short paragraph, it communicates a comprehensive portrait of Alicia and the teacher's concerns for her. The other is that it communicates competence and thoughtfulness on the part of the teacher and establishes her as an advocate for Alicia.

Exercise

Consider a student about whom you have concerns and answer the six questions above. In what ways do the answers clarify your thinking about the student? What do you think the next action should be?

Going Forward

This chapter focused on the recognition aspect of teachers' involvement in their students' mental health. As we have discussed, teachers must be more involved in helping students to access support and care. Recognition is the first step in teachers' becoming effective advocates and gateway providers. In the following chapter, we focus on the "respond" aspect of this role. Responding to students with mental health challenges involves knowing how to have conversations with students that are supportive and facilitate the process of accessing needed help.

Takeaways

- Teachers play an essential role in an initial screening and referral process.
- Mental health problems tend to express themselves in three broad dimensions: (1) internalizing problems, (2) externalizing problems, and (3) thought disorders.
- To understand whether a problem is serious, teachers can use a series of questions that include:
  - What, specifically, is the student doing or not doing that troubles you?
  - How have these behaviors impacted the student's learning? How do you think these behaviors impact the student socially?
  - Do these behaviors seem typical or atypical?
  - Are these behaviors developmentally appropriate?
  - What would the consequences of these behaviors be later in the child's development?
  - How intense are these problems?
    - ☐ How long?
    - ☐ How frequent?
    - ☐ Rate on a scale of 1 to 10.

- What do you think the student is feeling? What do you think the student is thinking about your class, school, and his or her life in general?
- What is going on in a student's life that might contribute to these behaviors?
- Who is this student connected to in a supportive way?

References

Achenbach, T. M., & Edelbrock, C. S. (1984). Psychopathology of childhood. *Annual Review of Psychology, 35,* 227–256.

Adelman, H. S., & Taylor, L. (2012). Mental health in schools: Moving in new directions. *Contemporary School Psychology, 16,* 9–18.

American Academy of Pediatrics, Committee on School Health. (2004). Policy statement. School-based mental health services. *Pediatrics, 13*(6), 1839–1845.

American Psychiatric Association (2013). *The diagnostic and statistical manual of mental disorders* (5th ed.). Author.

Ballard, K. L., Sander, M. A., & Klimes-Dougan, B. (2014). School-related and social–emotional outcomes of providing mental health services in schools. *Community Mental Health Journal, 50*(2), 145.

Barkley, R. (Ed.). (2006). *Attention-deficit hyperactivity disorder: A handbook for diagnosis and treatment* (3rd ed.). Guilford Press.

Bradshaw, C. P., Buckley, J. A., & Ialongo, N. S. (2008). School-based service utilization among urban children with early onset educational and mental health problems: The squeaky wheel phenomenon. *School Psychology Quarterly, 23*(2), 169–189. https://doi.org/10.1037/1045-3830.23.2.169

Brown, A. (2012). *With poverty comes depression, more than other illnesses.* https://news.gallup.com/poll/158417/poverty-comes-depression-illness.aspx

Bruchmüller, K., Margraf, J., & Schneider, S. (2012). Is ADHD diagnosed in accord with diagnostic criteria? Overdiagnosis and influence of client gender on diagnosis. *Journal of Consulting and Clinical Psychology, 80*(1), 128–138.

Burns, B. J., Costello, E. J., Angold, A., Tweed, D., Stangl, D., Farmer, E. M., & Erkanli, A. (1995). Children's mental health service use across service sectors. *Health Affairs, 14,* 147–159.

Caspi, A., Houts, R. M., Belsky, D. W., Goldman-Mellor, S. J., Harrington, H., Israel, S., Meier, M. H., Ramrakha, S., Shalev, I., Poulton, R., & Moffitt, T. E. (2014). *The p factor: One general psychopathology factor in the structure of psychiatric disorders?* https://doi-org.libproxy.chapman.edu/10.1177/2167702613497473

Cokley, K., Cody, B., Smith, L., Beasley, S., Miller, K. I. S., Hurst, A., Awosogba, O., Stone, S., & Jackson, S. (2015). Bridge over troubled waters: Meeting the mental health needs of Black students. *Phi Delta Kappan, 96*(4), 40–45.

Copeland, W. E., Angold, A., Shanahan, L., & Costello, E. J. (2014). Longitudinal patterns of anxiety from childhood to adulthood: The great smoky mountains study. *Journal of the American Academy of Child & Adolescent Psychiatry, 53*(1), 21–33.

Costello, E. J., Angold, A., Burns, B. J., Stangl, D. K., Tweed, D. L., Erkanli, A., & Worthman, C. M. (1996). The great smoky mountains study of youth: Goals, design, methods, and the prevalence of DSM-III-R disorders. *Archives of General Psychiatry, 53*, 1129–1136.

Costello, E. J., Erkanli, A., & Angold, A. (2006). Is there an epidemic of child or adolescent depression? *Journal of Child Psychology and Psychiatry, 47*(12), 1263–1271.

Costello, E. J., Mustillo, S., Erkanli, A., Keeler, G., & Angold, A. (2003). Prevalence and development of psychiatric disorders in childhood and adolescence. *Archives of General Psychiatry, 60*, 837–844.

Cunningham, J., & Suldo, S. (2014). Accuracy of teachers in identifying elementary school students who report at-risk levels of anxiety and depression. *School Mental Health, 6*(4), 237–250.

Dowdy, E., Doane, K., Eklund, K., & Dever, B. V. (2013). A comparison of teacher nomination and screening to identify behavioral and emotional risk within a sample of underrepresented students. *Journal of Emotional & Behavioral Disorders, 21*(2), 127–137.

Farmer, R. F., Seeley, J. R., Kosty, D. B., & Lewinsohn, P. M. (2009). Refinements in the hierarchical structure of externalizing psychiatric disorders: Patterns of lifetime liability from mid-adolescence through early adulthood. *Journal of Abnormal Psychology (1965), 118*(4), 699–710.

Gabbay, V., Johnson, A. R., Alonso, C. M., Evans, L. K., Babb, J. S., & Klein, R. G. (2015). Anhedonia, but not irritability, is associated with illness severity outcomes in adolescent major depression. *Journal of Child & Adolescent Psychopharmacology, 25*(3), 194–200. https://doi-org.libproxy.chapman.edu/10.1089/cap.2014.0105

Gay, Lesbian and Straight Education Network. (2014). *The 2013 National School Climate Survey—Executive summary*. Author.

Ghandour, R. M., Sherman, L. J., Vladutiu, C. J., Ali, M. M., Lynch, S. E., Bitsko, R. H., & Blumberg, S. J. (2019). Prevalence and treatment of depression, anxiety, and conduct problems in US children. *The Journal of Pediatrics*, *206*, 256–267.

Greytak, E. A., Kosciw, J. G., & Diaz, E. M. (2009). *Harsh realities: The experiences of transgender youth in our nation's schools*. GLSEN.

Harvard Civil rights Project, C. M. (2000). *Opportunities suspended: The devastating consequences of zero tolerance and school discipline policies. Report from a National Summit on Zero Tolerance [Proceedings] (Washington, DC, June 15–16, 2000)*.

Kahneman, D. (2011). *Thinking, fast and slow*. New York: Farrar, Straus, and Giroux.

Kaplan, D. W., Calonge, B. N., Guernsey, B. P., & Hanrahan, M. B. (1998). Managed care and school-based health centers: Use of health services. *Archives of Pediatrics and Adolescent Medicine*, *1*, 25–33.

Kessler, R. C., Berglund, P. A., Bruce, M. L., Koch, J. R., Laska, E. M., Leaf, P. J., Manderscheid, R. W., Rosenheck, R. A., Walters, E. E., & Wang, P. S. (2001). The prevalence and correlates of untreated serious mental illness. *Health Services Research*, *36*, 987–1007.

Kessler, R. C., Ruscio, A. M., Shear, K., & Wittchen, H. U. (2009). Epidemiology of anxiety disorders. *Behavioral Neurobiology of Anxiety and Its Treatment*, 21–35.

Kotov, R., Ruggero, C. J., Krueger, R. F., Watson, D., Yuan, Q., & Zimmerman, M. (2011). New dimensions in the quantitative classification of mental illness. *Archives of General Psychiatry*, *10*, 1003–1011.

Kunesh, C. E., & Noltemeyer, A. (2019). Understanding disciplinary disproportionality: Stereotypes shape pre-service teachers' beliefs about Black boys' behavior. *Urban Education*, *54*(4), 471–498.

Loades, M. E., & Mastroyannopoulou, K. (2010). Teachers' recognition of children's mental health problems. *Child & Adolescent Mental Health*, *15*(3), 150–156.

Merikangas, K., Nakamura, E. F., Kessler, R. C., & Macher, J. P. (2010). Epidemiology of mental disorders in children and adolescents. *Child and Adolescent Psychiatry*, *11*(1), 7–20.

Munzer, T. G., Miller, A. L., Brophy-Herb, H. E., Peterson, K. E., Horodynski, M. A., Contreras, D., Sturza, J., Kaciroti, N., & Lumeng, J. C. (2018).

Characteristics associated with parent–teacher concordance on child behavior problem ratings in low-income preschoolers. *Academic Pediatrics, 18*(4), 452–459.

Muroff, J., & Ross, A. (2011). Social disability and impairment in childhood anxiety. In *Handbook of child and adolescent anxiety disorders* (pp. 457–478). Springer Science + Business Media.

Mychailyszyn, M. P., Mendez, J. L., & Kendall, P. C. (2010). School functioning in youth with and without anxiety disorders: Comparisons by diagnosis and comorbidity. *School Psychology Review, 39*(1), 106–121.

Nail, J. E., Christofferson, J., Ginsburg, G. S., Drake, K., Kendall, P. C., McCracken, J. T., Birmaher, B., Walkup, J. T., Compton, S. N., Keeton, C., & Sakolsky, D. (2015). Academic impairment and impact of treatments among youth with anxiety disorders. *Child & Youth Care Forum: Journal of Research and Practice in Children's Services, 44*(3), 327–342.

Papandrea, K., & Winefield, H. (2011). It's not just the squeaky wheels that need the oil: Examining Teachers' views on the disparity between referral rates for students with internalizing versus externalizing problems. *School Mental Health, 3*(4), 222–235.

Rapee, R. M., Schniering, C. A., & Hudson, J. L. (2009). Anxiety disorders during childhood and adolescence: Origins and treatment. *Annual Review of Clinical Psychology, 5*, 311.

Rothì, D. M., Leavey, G., & Best, R. (2008). On the front-line: Teachers as active observers of pupils' mental health. *Teaching and Teacher Education, 24*(5), 1217–1231.

Rutter, M. (2003). Poverty and child mental health: Natural experiments and social causation. *JAMA, 290*(15), 2063–2064. https://doi.org/10.1001/jama.290.15.2063

Splett, J. W., Garzona, M., Gibson, N., Wojtalewicz, D., Raborn, A., & Reinke, W. M. (2019). Teacher recognition, concern, and referral of children's internalizing and externalizing behavior problems. *School Mental Health: A Multidisciplinary Research and Practice Journal, 11*(2), 228–239.

Stewart, J. G., Esposito, E. C., Glenn, C. R., Gilman, S. E., Pridgen, B., Gold, J., & Auerbach, R. P. (2016). Adolescent self-injurers: Comparing non-ideators, suicide ideators, and suicide attempters. *Journal of Psychiatric Research, 84*, 102–112.

Stiffman, A. R., Stelk, W., Horwitz, S. M., Evans, M. E., Outlaw, F. H., & Atkins, M. (2010). A public health approach to children's mental health services: Possible solutions to current service inadequacies.

Administration and Policy in Mental Health and Mental Health Services Research, 37(1–2), 120–124.

Stiffman, A. R., Striley, C., Horvath, V. E., Hadley-Ives, E., Polgar, M., Elze, D., & Pescarino, R. (2001). Organizational context and provider perception as determinants of mental health service use. *The Journal of Behavioral Health Services & Research, 28*(2), 188–204.

Strein, W., Hoagwood, K., & Cohn, A. (2003). School psychology: A public health perspective I. Prevention, populations, and systems change. *Journal of School Psychology, 41*, 23–38. https://doi.org/10.1016/S0022-4405(02)00142-5

Vázquez, A. L., & Villodas, M. T. (2019). Racial/ethnic differences in caregivers' perceptions of the need for and utilization of adolescent psychological counseling and support services. *Cultural Diversity & Ethnic Minority Psychology, 25*(3), 323–330.

Whitcomb, S. A., & Merrell, K. W. (2013). *Behavioral, social, and emotional assessment of children and adolescents* (4th ed.). Routledge/Taylor & Francis Group.

Wiley, D. C., & Cory, A. C. (2013). *Encyclopedia of school health*. Sage.

Yang, L., Zhao, Y., Wang, Y., Liu, L., Zhang, X., Li, B., & Cui, R. (2015). The effects of psychological stress on depression. *Current Neuropharmacology, 13*(4), 494–504.

5

Respond

Supportive Communication Skills for Teachers

This chapter focuses on the skills needed for teachers to have supportive interactions with distressed students. These skills build on the concepts discussed in previous chapters, particularly resilience and the fundamental importance of relationships to learning and, notably, on attitudes toward students. In the field of counseling, this attitude has been described as a *stance* of *not knowing*, which Anderson and Goolishian (1992) define as a "general attitude or stance in which the therapist's actions communicate an abundant, genuine curiosity" (p. 29).

A stance of not knowing means that we do not respond to students' distress by immediately giving advice but, rather, listen patiently while being respectful of the student's perspective, even if it doesn't quite make sense to us yet. The abundant curiosity mentioned by Anderson and Goolishian (1992) leads us to ask questions that allow students to explain their perspective and what they need before we try to problem solve. This chapter builds on this perspective by focusing on skills that will make these conversations easier and more helpful.

Of course, we are not expecting teachers to be counselors or psychotherapists. As psychologist and philosopher William

DOI: 10.4324/9780367810269-5

James (1958) stated, "The worst thing that can happen to a good teacher is to get a bad conscience about her profession because she feels herself hopeless as a psychologist" (p. 27). Nevertheless, we also understand that there are many occasions in which teachers are approached by students—often before anybody else—and put in the position of responding. As noted, in this chapter, we seek to make those conversations more supportive and helpful and, to this end, draw upon the knowledge and skills of effective counselors and psychologists with the understanding that these are also the communication skills of good teachers.

A Supportive Stance

The ability to apply the skills needed to listen attentively and carefully is supported by a stance of not knowing. The foundations of a stance of not knowing include empathy, compassion, trust, respect, and curiosity. Before we present the specific skills that allow for supportive conversations, we will briefly discuss each of these qualities.

Empathy and Compassion

Carl Rogers (1980), considered the founder of what is often called *client-centered therapy*, argued that empathy, or the "sensitive ability and willingness to understand the client's thoughts, feelings, and struggles from the client's point of view" (p. 85) is a key component of successful counseling. Rogers (1983) also stated that empathy is critical for teaching and learning, stating that, when a teacher "has the sensitive awareness of the way the process of education and learning seem to the student, then the likelihood of significant learning is increased" (p. 125). Empathy is critical for education and learning because teachers must understand what learning is like for the students.

Rogers (1957) noted that empathy has a cognitive or meaning aspect and an affective or emotional aspect. This means that, although perfect empathy is rare, at best, if we are to have at least an imperfect understanding of someone else's experience, we must understand the meaning that the person gives to experience and the related emotions that they experiences. If teachers lack the cognitive aspect of empathy, they will have difficulty understanding what someone else is thinking. If they lack the affective dimension of empathy, they will have trouble understanding someone else's feelings, and, more importantly, they will have difficulty with feeling for others. Without these two aspects of empathy, the limbic resonance discussed in Chapter 3 is not possible. Remember that limbic resonance is a way of expressing how the brains of two people connect. It is impossible to overstate how important limbic resonance is for learning and change to occur.

Although critical for learning and change, empathy, as we have defined it, can be passive. Compassion extends empathy to include an understanding of someone's suffering and the desire to act to alleviate pain (Bibeau et al., 2016). Although empathy is essential to having successful social interactions of all types, not just conversations with distressed students, empathy alone can potentially lead to increased negative emotions on the part of the person who listens and shares in someone else's pain (Klimecki et al., 2014). This increase in negative affect or distress in the face of someone else's suffering appears to be reduced by compassion. For example, Klimecki and colleagues found that short-term empathy training increased negative affect in response to videos of others' suffering. Follow-up training in compassion reversed the negative emotions that arose from empathy for someone else's pain and increased positive affect. As Klimecki et al. stated, "The generation of compassion focuses on strengthening positive affect, while not ignoring the presence of suffering or changing the negative reality" (p. 877). They argue that this ability to be present and open to someone's suffering may be a prerequisite to helping behaviors.

Respect

Respect for a student's viewpoint follows from empathy and compassion. The notion of respect is related to Rogers' (1957) concept of unconditional positive regard, defined as "no conditions of acceptance, no feeling of 'I like you only if you are thus and so'" (p. 98). This acceptance of someone else does not mean that teachers think everything that students are thinking or feeling is accurate and appropriate; instead, it means that teachers respect students enough to allow them the room to express themselves without communicating judgment. Respect encourages trust, which, in turn, facilitates a sense of security in a relationship.

Curiosity

In addition to empathy, compassion, trust, and respect, a stance of not knowing implies curiosity about someone's viewpoint. Having a sense of curiosity about someone relieves the listener from having to take immediate action to solve a problem and allows students the space to express what is on their minds more fully, which, in turn, opens up the potential for students to figure out things for themselves. Again, teachers are not psychotherapists, but merely listening and being curious about a student's perspective on life can, by itself, have a powerful impact on a student's well-being. Rogers (1957) connected listening and helping his clients: "I discovered that simply listening to my client, very attentively, was an important way of being helpful. So, when I was in doubt as to what I should do, in some active way, I listened" (p. 2). In the next section, we discuss the flow of a conversation from beginning to end as well as the listening and communication skills that allow teachers to express the qualities of empathy, compassion, respect, and curiosity.

Having Supportive Conversations with Students

Anderson and Goolishian (1992) coined the term *stance of not knowing*, but De Jong and Kim Berg (2013) appear to have been the first to use *skills for not knowing* to describe the specific listening skills that underlie this stance. We prefer skills for not knowing over other possible ways of describing these skills because this term clarifies that the listening skills crucial to having supportive conversations with students do not exist in isolation but, instead, arise from the qualities discussed above. Skills for not knowing are on a continuum from nonverbal behaviors that communicate attentive listening to active skills, such as reflecting thoughts and feeling or asking questions (Hass, 2018). In the following discussion, we move from learning how to "not to duck" when approached by a distressed student to gently asking questions that allow students to tell their stories.

How Not to Duck
A first step to having supportive conversations with students is to learn how "not to duck," or not emotionally move away from their distress. Teachers are typically comfortable when approached about academic issues, but they can be taken aback when students approach them to express emotional distress over something happening in their lives. To prepare to have a conversation about students' emotional experience, we suggest the strategy of *breathe, look, and remind*, as described below.

To begin, take a deep breath. Even one deep breath will lower tension in the body and turn down the sympathetic nervous system. After a deep breath, bring yourself into the moment and prepare to focus your attention on the student in front of you. For students who are looking for emotional support from an adult, there is almost nothing worse than for the adult to be distracted while the students are trying to express themselves. Lastly, remind yourself that your job is not to solve the problem the student brings to you. It is your job to listen and, if appropriate, connect the student to the resources they need. You might remind yourself of Rogers' statement, "All I have to do is listen."

Beginning a Conversation: "I'm Ready to Talk with You"
Once you are ready, a second step is to open the conversation with students by offering an invitation to talk about whatever is on their minds. These invitations can be as simple as saying, "Hi, what's going on?" or "What did you want to talk about, John?" These statements, although simple, serve multiple purposes. They help to kick start what might be an awkward conversation for the students to start on their own, even though they may have initiated the conversation. A distressed student may have decided to seek help, but it remains challenging to start those conversations. An invitation to talk provides simple scaffolding for students to begin to speak about what is on their mind.

Compliments

Compliments, especially when given by a trusted adult, can be a powerful way of facilitating a more open conversation with a student. In Chapter 1, we discussed the importance of a strengths perspective. Genuine compliments communicate that a teacher has "seen" a student and, even more important, sees something beyond the student's current struggles. Compliments make it more likely that students will be open to advice or suggestions when the time is right to offer them. They also can increase a sense of hope and even empowerment. Students with mental health problems are often very aware of their struggles. A teacher who offers a compliment in a conversation, to paraphrase singer and songwriter Leonard Cohen, opens a crack for the light to get in.

Waiting, Attending, and Minimal Encouragers: "I'm Listening"

Listening begins with nonverbal attending and waiting (Hass, 2018). Similar to not ducking, waiting involves being patient with pauses and silence. Often, out of anxiety or a rush to solve a problem, we fill the space in a conversation with questions or suggestions, interrupting students' thinking and pushing them to respond before they are ready. The concept of increasing wait time following a question is not new to teachers. As an instructional strategy, allowing a few seconds more after asking a question in the classroom increases participation and reduces disruptive behaviors. It also improves the fullness and complexity of the answer (Rowe, 1986). Pausing after asking a distressed student a question can be thought of as emotional wait time. Like its instructional equivalent, emotional wait time helps students to feel less pressure to respond and allows them the time to provide more thoughtful responses to our questions.

Nonverbal attending can be divided into specific behaviors, such as facing someone; having an open, relaxed posture; and maintaining appropriate eye contact (Carkhuff & Anthony, 1979). These and other subtle, nonverbal behaviors constitute the communication of "physical and psychological presence" (Egan, 1975). These behaviors set the stage for the verbal interactions that follow and have been described as the background music in a movie that, although we may not be conscious of it, influences our emotional experience significantly (Young, 2001). Being present and attentive with a student sets the stage for the expression of curiosity through questions and other ways to encourage students to express themselves more fully.

Minimal encouragers are the small verbal gestures that friends use in conversation. They are verbal but typically limited to one word or sometimes just a sound. Examples include "oh," "okay," "hmmm," or "wow." They can also involve repeating a keyword or words that someone uses. These behaviors encourage continued conversation by indicating agreement, acknowledgment, or understanding (Hill, 1978).

Paraphrasing and Summarizing: "I Understand"

In their discussion of skills for not knowing, De Jong and Kim Berg (2013) describe paraphrasing and summarizing as critical tools for communicating empathy, compassion, and respect. Skillful paraphrasing involves distilling the essence of what someone has said. It may include content, meaning, and feelings. Paraphrasing often will include at least a subtle interpretation or reframing. In contrast, summarizing involves restating what someone has said. Summarizing and paraphrasing also offer an opportunity for students to affirm teachers' understanding. Asking for a confirmation of understanding can then be an opportunity to empower the student by communicating that what the student says is essential. It also gives students a chance to edit their remarks, leading to a fuller, more accurate picture of their experience.

Questions, Implied Questions, and Conversational Prompts: "I'm Curious. What's Going On?"

Skills such as nonverbal attending, minimal encouragers, summarizing, and paraphrasing communicate empathy, compassion, and respect. These build a foundation for curiosity, which is typically expressed via questions or conversational prompts. Questions and conversational prompts can help gather more information about someone's perspective and communicate that one is listening carefully. When asking questions, it is often helpful to request permission before asking. Requesting permission expresses respect for students' autonomy and, at the same time, makes it more likely they will give that permission and answer your questions.

Conversational prompts are requests for someone to provide more information, such as "Please tell me more about that." Questions can be closed- or open-ended. Closed questions are usually answered with a yes or no. When asked closed-ended questions, older students will often voluntarily provide more information than is required to answer the question. Children, however, are more likely to stick to the parameters of the question and offer shorter, unelaborated answers (Lyon, 2014).

Interestingly, research on interviewing child witnesses in the field of forensic psychology suggests that open-ended questions and conversational prompts lead to more detailed and accurate information than do more directive, closed-ended questions (Cederborg et al., 2000). Whether questions are open or closed, it is essential to remember that too many can cause students to feel interrogated. Although there are times in a conversation with students when it is appropriate to express curiosity by asking questions about their experiences, it is best to intersperse questions with liberal amounts of summarizing and paraphrasing.

Implied questions are indirect requests for more information that involve thinking aloud using tentative language, such as "could it," "maybe it is," or "I wonder if." This wondering aloud works best when it comes from a stance of not knowing and genuine curiosity. It is a way of placing your thoughts on the table without the pressure of a direct question. One caution is not to use phrases such as "Do you think" or "Do you know?" because they often come across as a kind of mind-reading test. The student knows you have a thought or idea and can then feel pressured to guess the answer.

In addition to conversational prompts, open-ended questions, and implied questions, it is often helpful to use two other kinds of questions: scaling and relationship. We discussed a type of scaling question in Chapter 4, when we addressed the issue of intensity as part of a way to answer the question, "Do these behaviors seem typical or atypical?" The question provides an estimate of how severe or intense a problem is from the teacher's perspective. Scaling questions can provide helpful information without the expectation that students will offer much detail. For example, a teacher might say to a student, "Wow, that is tough. On a scale of one to ten, how bad are things right now?"

Relationship questions can broaden a conversation by imaginatively bringing in the viewpoint of someone important in a student's life. They also have the advantage of subtly encouraging students to consider someone else's view of their situation, which can open up space for them to see the situation differently. Examples of relationship questions are, "If your English teacher were here, what would she say about how you are doing in class?" or "If your mom were here, what would she say?"

Concluding a Conversation: "Here Are the Next Steps"

It is important to understand that you should not expect to resolve a student's concerns in a short conversation. It is likely not possible, not only for you but for anybody. As a teacher, your first goal is to listen well enough for the student to feel supported and understood. A second goal is to connect the student to school or community resources, something we discuss in-depth in Chapter 7. A last potential goal is to offer accommodations to make the student's life easier in your class. The final step in the flow of a conversation with a student who potentially has mental health problems is to summarize what you have heard and the next steps. You can think of this in three parts:

1. This is what you said.
2. This is who I am going to talk to about getting you the help you need.
3. This is what I can do to help.

The last part is optional because there may be nothing that can be done in the short term to help. It is also not necessary for you, as the teacher, to have ready-made ideas. It is often better to let students take the lead in offering suggestions about what they think is needed. Asking, "What do you think would help?" and encouraging the student to respond can be a powerful driver of autonomy and confidence.

Skills for Not Knowing in Action

The dialogue below is between Aaron, the 15-year-old transgender student we discussed in Chapter 4, and his health teacher, Ms. Campbell. Aaron is irritable and cranky with his peers and does little homework, although he finishes most of his classwork. You may remember that Aaron had a conversation with his health teacher, Ms. Campbell. The dialogue below recreates this conversation and illustrates the skills we have discussed so far.

Ms. C:	"Hey, Aaron, thanks for taking the time to talk with me."
Aaron:	"Sure, … my sister is coming to pick me up in about 20 minutes; will that be okay?"
Ms. C:	"No problem. Well, first, I wanted to say that you are doing an excellent job of getting your work done in class. It seems like it isn't very hard for you. Am I right? [*compliment*]
Aaron:	"No, it is not so hard."
Ms. C:	"Okay, that's good. So, listen, the other thing I wanted to talk with you about is that it just seems you are not very happy. I guess I am wondering if you are okay." [*the last sentence is an implied question*]
Aaron:	"Well, I am better than I was before."
Ms. C:	"Good. How are you better, do you think?" [*open-ended question*]
Aaron:	"A while back, I was in the hospital because I wanted to … (pause) … to hurt myself. I don't feel like that anymore. Also, I am back in school … part of the time."
Ms. C:	"Okay, so you don't want to hurt yourself anymore … glad to hear that … and you think it is good you are back in school part-time." [*paraphrase*] Okay, can you

	tell me more about what is going on now? [*conversational prompt*]
Aaron:	"I don't know … it is hard. I am tired all the time, and people make me mad."
Ms. C:	"Wow, okay." [*minimal encourager*]
Aaron:	"Yeah, I don't want to get mad, but it feels like I can't help myself. Also, you know, I'm trans, and sometimes people say stuff. I don't know; most people are cool, but some of them are just a-holes, you know."
Ms. C:	"It really does sound hard." [*paraphrase, but focused on feelings*]
Aaron:	"Yeah." (Aaron looks down and seems sad)
Ms. C:	"Can I ask you another question, Aaron?" [*requesting permission*]
Aaron:	"Sure."
Ms. C:	"On a scale of 1 to 10, with 1 being things are as bad as they could possibly be, and 10 is that things are as good as they could be, what number would you give yourself now?" [*scaling question*]
Aaron:	"I don't know; about a 6, I guess."
Ms. C:	"Wow, that's better than I thought. You are hanging in there despite everything. Good job." [*compliment*]
Aaron:	"Oh, okay. That's good, I guess."
Ms. C:	"What about my class, Aaron? [*open-ended question*] As I said, I know you can do the work. What could we do to get you to do a little more homework?" [*open-ended question*]
Aaron:	"I don't know. I just feel too tired when I get home to do all of it … maybe I could do something. Would that help?"
Ms. C:	"Sure, yeah, that would help. I know you said your sister was coming to pick you up, so we should wrap it up. What I got was that things are better than they were before, but you feel tired and cranky with the other students in the class. I told you that you are doing pretty well with classwork but not so well with homework. [*summarizing*] What I think would be best is that I talk to the school counselor,

	Ms. Rodriguez, to see if we can get you some more help. Maybe some counseling to help you feel better. Would it be okay if I talk with her about that?"
Aaron:	"Okay, I know her a little. She seems okay."
Ms. C:	"Great. Also, I think, for the homework, you just pick something. One thing you think you can do and do that. We'll see how that goes. How does that sound?"
Aaron:	"Sounds okay."
Ms. C:	"Well, Aaron, thanks for talking with me [*compliment*]. I know that isn't always easy. I'll see you in class tomorrow and let you know what Ms. Rodriguez says."
Aaron:	"All right, see you later."

In this case, Ms. Campbell initiated the conversation. She opened with a compliment and a simple implied question about her concerns. During the conversation, Ms. Campbell used several of the skills we discussed above, including minimal encouragers, compliments, conversational prompts, paraphrasing, summarizing, implied questions, open-ended questions (as well as a few appropriate closed-ended questions), and a scaling question. She ended with a summary of what they had talked about and what she planned to do. It is important to note that she stopped to ask Aaron whether it was okay if she took those actions at each step in her final statement. In a sense, she was asking permission. Our experience is that, in almost all cases, when asked permission, students will say yes because being asked implies a sense of autonomy and choice. If Aaron had said no to the idea of talking to Ms. Rodriguez for some reason, Ms. Campbell might have had to adopt a gently more assertive stance, as seen below.

> I understand that you don't want help from Ms. Rodriguez, but I have to talk with someone about what is going on. I want to help, but I am a teacher, and I can't give you all the help you need. I know you don't want me

to talk with her, and I don't want to upset you, but would you go along with it, even if you don't really like it?

Our experience is that much of what passes for resistance and a lack of cooperation comes from students fighting for a sense of independence in situations in which it feels like that is being taken away from them. The trust and sense of mutual respect that emerge from a conversation in which a student feels deeply listened to make cooperation more likely. It also helps students with mental health issues to feel less isolated and alone in working with their challenges. More than that, as we have learned, these kinds of conversations and the relationships that come from them can causes changes in the brain and lead to meaningful behavioral change. Although in the long term, these changes may have to continue in counseling or psychotherapy, it is well within the capacity of teachers to begin the process.

Conclusion

In this chapter, we have explored the personal qualities and communication skills that help teachers to have supportive conversations with students when they are upset or distressed or simply want to talk about something in their lives. As we have said, teachers are not therapists, but they can have conversations with students that are helpful and provide the context for change. Lewis et al. (2001) call this *limbic revision* a mutual influencing of two brains that stabilizes emotions and opens the door to learning. In the next chapter, we further explore what we have learned in this chapter in the context of the extremes of life, including suicide, crisis, and trauma.

Takeaways

- ♦ Empathy, compassion, and respect are the foundations to listening carefully and having supportive conversations with students.

- Skills that support careful listening include giving compliments, paraphrasing, and asking skillful questions.
- Concluding a conversation includes:
  - This is what you said.
  - This is who I am going to talk to about getting you the help you need.
  - This is what I can do to help.

References

Anderson, H., & Goolishian, H. (1992). The client is the expert: A not-knowing approach to therapy. In S. McNamee, & K. Gergen (Eds.), *Social construction and the therapeutic process* (pp. 25–39). Sage.

Bibeau, M., Dionne, F., & Leblanc, J. (2016). Can compassion meditation contribute to the development of Psychotherapists' empathy? A review. *Mindfulness*, 7(1), 255–263.

Carkhuff, R. R., & Anthony, W. A. (1979). *The skills of helping*. Human Development Press.

Cederborg, A., Orbach, Y., & Sternberg, K. J. (2000). Investigative interviews of child witnesses in Sweden. *Child Abuse & Neglect*, 24(10), 1355–1361.

De Jong, P., & Kim Berg, I. (2013). *Interviewing for solutions*. Brooks/Cole, Cengage Learning.

Egan, G. (1975). *The skilled helper: A model for systematic helping and interpersonal relating*. Brooks/Cole.

Hass, M. (2018). *Interviewing for assessment: A practical guide for school counselors and school psychologists*. John Wiley & Sons.

Hill, C. E. (1978). Development of a counselor verbal response category. *Journal of Counseling Psychology*, 25(5), 461–468. https://doi.org/10.1037/0022-0167.25.5.461

James, W. (1958). *Talks to teachers on psychology: And to students of life's ideals*. W. W. Norton.

Klimecki, O. M., Leiberg, S., Ricard, M., & Singer, T. (2014). *Differential pattern of functional brain plasticity after compassion and empathy training*. https://doi-org.libproxy.chapman.edu/10.1093/scan/nst060

Lewis, T., Amini, F., & Lannon, R. (2001). *A general theory of love*. Knopf Doubleday.

Lyon, T. D. (2014). Interviewing children. *Annual Review of Law & Social Science*, *10*(5), 73–89.
Rogers, C. R. (1957). Necessary and sufficient conditions of therapeutic personality change. *Journal of Consulting Psychology*, *21*, 95–103.
Rogers, C. R. (1980). *A way of being*. Houghton Mifflin.
Rogers, C. R. (1983). *Freedom to learn*. Charles E. Merrill.
Rowe, M. B. (1986). Wait time: Slowing down may be a way of speeding up! *Journal of Teacher Education*, *37*, 43–50. https://doiorg.libproxy.chapman.edu/10.1177/002248718603700110
Young, M. E. (2001). *Learning the art of helping: Building blocks and techniques* (2nd ed.). Merrill/Prentice-Hall.

6

Respond

Teachers' Role in Understanding and Responding to Crises and Trauma

Chapter 5 presented the qualities and skills needed for teachers to have supportive interactions with distressed students. In this chapter, we discuss the application of these skills to crises and trauma. As background to this discussion, we consider what constitutes a crisis, how children typically react to a crisis event, what the more severe reactions to a crisis or trauma look like in children of different ages, and what factors make children more vulnerable. Later in this chapter, we present a continuum of actions that can be taken when responding to a crisis. We also discuss the long-term effects of stress on children who experience developmental trauma.

Knowledge of crisis and trauma is essential for teachers. This is, in part, because children are an especially vulnerable group. Despite the common belief that children are more resilient than adults and can bounce back from a crisis quickly, in most cases, children are more vulnerable than adults to crisis events (Barenbaum et al., 2004). Another reason for teachers to learn how to respond to crisis events is that crisis events often produce a dramatic increase in students with mental health needs. Further, many students do not receive care due to limited resources, resulting in long-term mental health problems (McCabe et al., 2014). In a crisis event, teachers are considered first responders and, when trained, can provide care that mitigates some of the adverse consequences of crisis events. As we have argued in previous chapters, although teachers are not mental health professionals, they can provide effective and needed support during and after a crisis.

Introduction to Crisis and Trauma

A crisis event is one that is perceived to be extremely negative, uncontrollable, and unpredictable (Brock et al., 2016). The experience of extreme negativity is often associated with the threat of harm or death (Bufka et al., 2020), and a crisis event overwhelms a person's capacity to cope (Gilliland & James, 1997; Slaikeu, 1990). The kinds of events that can constitute a crisis include natural disasters, such as earthquakes or floods, as well as human-caused events, such as suicides, school shootings, and aggression, that lead to injury or death (Brock et al., 2009). Crisis events can have a variety of negative consequences, and sometimes these adverse outcomes are severe and long-term. At the same time, if those who experience a crisis can cope with the aftermath successfully, they often emerge with greater confidence, improved relationships with others, appreciation of new possibilities, and new understandings of meaning and purpose (Gilliland & James, 1997; Tedeschi, 2020; Tedeschi & Moore, 2016)

The impact of a crisis event can be influenced by several factors, including characteristics of the event, physical and emotional proximity of those involved, and the interplay of risk and resilience in individuals. Events that involve human aggression or interpersonal violence are more likely to lead to severe reactions, such as post-traumatic stress disorder (PTSD; American Psychiatric Association, 2013; Brock et al., 2016). The extreme levels of aggression found in war or even smaller-scale violent conflicts can lead to levels of PTSD that range from 22% to 98% of children assessed (Barenbaum et al., 2004). Natural disasters tend to be less traumatic than are human-caused events, but their potential to cause trauma increases when they are unpredictable, lead to multiple injuries or death, or continue for an extended time (Brock et al., 2016).

In addition to the characteristics of crisis events, there is also a strong relationship between the degree of exposure to a crisis event and the severity of someone's reaction (Brock et al., 2016). Exposure can be physical or emotional. Physical exposure exists on a continuum that ranges from being a direct victim of the event to someone who was out of the area at the time of the crisis. Several studies have found that the closer one is to a crisis event (e.g., direct victim, witness), the greater one's risk of trauma (Boxer & Sloan-Power, 2013; Lowe & Galea, 2017). This suggests that those at the most significant risk have been direct victims of violence, been otherwise injured, or require medical treatment. This higher level of risk makes sense, given that higher rates of PTSD are found in groups with direct exposure to violence, e.g., war veterans, survivors of sexual assault.

In addition to physical exposure, emotional exposure increases the risk of trauma. Like physical exposure, emotional exposure exists on a continuum from having a best friend or sibling killed or injured in a crisis event to not knowing the event's victims. Emotional proximity can also be about the event's location, such as a workplace or frequently visited site. In sum, one's perception of safety during a crisis event is related not only to actual exposure to the event but also to the emotional closeness that someone feels toward those most affected.

The interplay of risk and resilience that we discussed in Chapter 2 also plays a role in how children respond to a crisis. For example, children who have stronger attachments to supportive adults or have more robust networks of peer relationships will be less likely to have long-term negative consequences from a crisis event (McNally et al., 2003). In addition, personal characteristics, such as skill at problem solving, good self-regulation, feelings of self-efficacy, and a sense of faith or hope, buffer children and improve their ability to bounce back from a crisis (Masten, 2014).

Conversely, those who have limited social support or lack skilled problem solving or self-regulation are more vulnerable when faced with a crisis event. In addition, students who have experienced the stresses explored in the ACE study (Felitti et al., 1998) are more vulnerable to the adverse effects of a crisis. Further, higher rates of PTSD have been found in people who were previously physically or sexually abused (McNally et al., 2003). Pre-existing anxiety or depressive disorders also make it more likely that someone will experience symptoms of PTSD after a crisis.

Reactions to Crisis

In the aftermath of a crisis event, it is essential to not over-interpret or pathologize children's reactions, even though, as we noted above, a crisis event that overwhelms someone's ability to cope can have various negative consequences. Although concerning, some responses are typical and usually improve with time and minimal intervention in the short term. If reactions or symptoms persist for an extended time, they can develop into more serious challenges, such as PTSD or the internalizing and externalizing disorders discussed in Chapter 2.

Short-term reactions to a crisis event will vary by age and development. For example, it is typical for children or adolescents to feel anxious after a crisis event (Brock et al., 2016). In young children, this might manifest as more clinginess toward parents or teachers; crying; physical problems, such as headaches or stomachaches; and generalized fearfulness of the dark or being alone (National Institute of Mental Health, n.d.). Older children, between the ages of 6 and 11, also may be more fearful and have physical problems, such as headaches or stomachaches. They also may become more irritable or have difficulties with concentrating (National Institute of Mental Health, n.d.).

Although adolescents are beginning to develop adult-like cognitive abilities, they are still in the process of developing a sense of individual identity and independence. This developing identity is sometimes fragile, leaving them vulnerable to crisis events that disrupt their sense of safety and disturb their connections with others. These disruptions can lead to a foreshortened sense of the future. Adolescents with a foreshortened sense of the future has temporarily lost trust that things will work out over time or that their activities and projects are meaningful (Ratcliffe et al., 2014). Their specific reactions to a crisis can run the gamut of those described for younger children but also include moodiness, anxiety, difficulty concentrating, difficulty sleeping, and aggression (Gerson & Rappaport, 2013).

As we stated above, it is important to keep in mind that recovery from a crisis is the norm (National Institute of Mental Health, 2002). Due to the expectation of recovery, identification of severe post-crisis problems, such as PTSD, is typically made a month or more after the event (Cohen, 2010). Although most children and youth will be resilient in the face of a crisis, about a third of students will manifest longer-lasting and more severe reactions (Cohen, 2010; Kessler et al., 1995).

Early reactions that appear to be signs of a greater potential for longer-term problems include extreme anxiety or panic attacks (Cohen, 2010) and dissociative states (Brock et al., 2016). Severe anxiety can be debilitating and often has intense physical symptoms, such as a racing heart, sweating, chills, trembling, breathing problems, weakness or dizziness, chest pain, stomach pain, and nausea (American Psychiatric Association, 2013). Dissociation in children can also include feeling numb or as if they were standing outside of themselves, watching what is happening. Both reactions are especially troublesome because they significantly interfere with students' ability to function in life. In the next section, we discuss further the nature of trauma and how it manifests in students' thoughts, feelings, and behavior.

Trauma
Trauma is the enduring adverse impact of a crisis. The sense of being overwhelmed that follows a crisis can lead to feelings of helplessness (Gilliland & James, 1997; Slaikeu, 1990). The physical and psychological responses to feeling bereft of the ability

to cope with life can have enduring negative consequences for students if their trauma is not addressed.

There are two pathways to trauma. One is the result of the acute events of the kind discussed above. A second pathway results from chronic stress or multiple prolonged stressful events in childhood (van der Kolk, 2014). The consequences of this second pathway, sometimes called *complex developmental trauma* (Cook et al., 2005), are what schools and communities have attempted to address by utilizing trauma-informed or trauma-sensitive practices (Chafouleas et al., 2016; Substance Abuse and Mental Health Services Administration [SAMHSA], 2014).

These enduring consequences of trauma can take many forms but typically fall into three categories: hyperarousal, intrusion, and dissociation. Hyperarousal occurs when the nervous system, specifically, the reaction we call *fight or flight*, is chronically simulated (Herman, 1992). This overactivity of the fight or flight response can result in chronic anxiety, hypersensitivity to environmental stimuli, and sleep disturbances. According to Herman, the bodies of traumatized individuals "are always on the alert for danger" (p. 36).

In addition to hyperarousal, enduring trauma is often characterized by intrusive thoughts, feelings, or images related to the traumatic event that the person cannot seem to stop. Children may exhibit repetitive play that expresses aspects of the traumatic event or have frightening dreams (American Psychiatric Association, 2013). Pierre Janet, an early French researcher of trauma, referred to this as the *idée fixe*, or the fixed idea (Herman, 1992). These fixed ideas leave victims of trauma feeling unable to free themselves of intrusive memories of the traumatic event.

The main consequence of trauma is dissociation. Dissociation is the psychological equivalent of a state of physical shock and can include feeling detached, spaced out, numb, or as if disconnected from the body (American Psychiatric Association, 2013; Herman, 1992). Hyperarousal and dissociation can be seen as ways of coping with extraordinary experiences. Even repetitive play or frightening dreams can be viewed as a way of coping by the person's trying to figure out the meaning of an event. In fact, most, if not all, of the behaviors of a person who has been traumatized by an event or events can be interpreted as understandable responses to an abnormal situation. The following scenarios show how these primary symptoms of trauma might manifest in students of different ages.

> **Scenario 1: Hyperarousal**
>
> Sandy is a 9-year-old fourth-grade student. Recently, there was an active-shooter alert. The students in her class were sheltered in her classroom for two hours before she and the other students in her class were released to their parents or guardians after discovering that the alert was a false alarm. Sandy lives at home with her father, an older brother, and a younger sister. Her mother passed away about a year ago after struggling with a chronic illness. Since returning to school after the shooting incident, Sandy is easily startled and irritable with other students. At break, she stays near the classroom and doesn't want to go out on the playground. Sandy struggles to explain herself, and she begins to cry intensely when her teacher says she must go out and be with the other children during break.

Sandy's loss of her mother makes her more vulnerable to the stress of the threat implied by an active shooter alert. When she returns to school, her behaviors, such as being easily startled and irritable, suggest someone whose sympathetic nervous system is stuck in the "on" position. Another sign of hyperarousal includes her reluctance to be on the playground, a place where she perceives herself as more vulnerable. When the sympathetic nervous system is overactive, the parts of our brain that make plans, problem solves, and uses words to explain things are often unavailable, making it more difficult to control our emotions or describe what is happening to us. Thus, Sandy's response to being asked why she did not want to go on the playground is to feel overwhelmed and to cry.

> **Scenario 2: Dissociation**
>
> Chris is a 12-year-old sixth-grade student. His father was recently deported after a raid on his place of business, a garden supply store. Chris has talked to his father, who has returned to his family's home in Mexico, once but hasn't had any other contact. Chris's mother recently approached Chris's history teacher, Mr. Sanchez, to ask for help. According to Chris's mother, Chris is very close to his father, but he has not expressed any emotions about his father's deportation. At home, Chris has also been more withdrawn and spends most of his time in his room, playing video games. Mr. Sanchez, who was not aware of the deportation, said that he had noticed that Chris was not participating in class discussions or small-group activities. Mr. Sanchez also had noticed that Chris seemed a bit "spaced out" and was spending more time than usual looking at his phone. Later, when Mr. Sanchez spoke to Chris, the child avoided eye contact and said, "Everything is fine," and asked whether he could leave.

As discussed above, dissociation is the equivalent of a state of physical shock. Withdrawal, emotional numbness, and avoidance, or an inability to talk about an experience, are signs that the experience is too overwhelming to deal with and, therefore, has been cut off or compartmentalized from the rest of someone's experience (van der Kolk, 2014). Chris exhibits several signs that his father's sudden departure feels overwhelming to him, and he is coping by trying to keep these thoughts and feelings at a distance. Although the splitting from his experience of losing his father is perhaps the only way Chris currently knows to cope, unfortunately, it also leaves him cut off from other people and even himself.

> **Scenario 3: Intrusion**
>
> Yolanda is 15 years old and a junior in high school. She was recently riding in a car with her friends, and the driver, a close friend of hers, lost control of the vehicle and ran into a streetlamp post near the school. Yolanda was shaken up but did not receive any serious injuries. Her friend, the driver, was knocked unconscious when the airbags deployed. She was taken to the hospital and was released two days later. Since the accident, Yolanda has had nightmares that contain images from the accident. She refuses to ride in a car, and at school, Yolanda is having trouble concentrating because she keeps thinking about the accident and her friend repeatedly. In class, she seems distracted, anxious, and sometimes "spaced out."

Traumatic memories are different from typical memories. Typical memories are not static photo shots of an event but are malleable pieces integrated into the larger story that people tell about their lives. With typical memories, this story changes over time (van der Kolk, 2014). Traumatic memories are unchanging and stand apart from the narrative of one's life, and, as a result, traumatic memories often manifest as sensory experiences that might include visual images, sounds, smells, tastes, or physical sensations (Michael et al., 2005). Yolanda's traumatic memories intrude into her school life and her dreams, interfering with her ability to focus on schoolwork and sleep.

Information about crisis and trauma allows teachers to better understand what children are going through in the aftermath of an acute crisis or experience as they cope with the ongoing toxic stresses associated with developmental trauma. In the following section, we discuss what is involved in healing from trauma and apply this to how teachers can support children during a crisis or students who live with enduring consequences.

Healing Trauma

As we noted above, a crisis is defined, in part, by its ability to overwhelm a person's ability to cope. This disequilibrium has the potential for what Slaikeu (1990) calls a "radically positive or negative outcome" (p. 15). Above, we discussed the negative consequences of crises. The radically adverse outcome is often expressed in enduring symptoms of hyperarousal, dissociation, and intrusive thoughts that do not resolve themselves and increasingly intrude upon someone's ability to function in school and/or life.

More surprising is the finding that most people, including children, recover and regain their equilibrium, often at a higher level of functioning than before. Tedeschi (2020) describes four elements of post-traumatic growth: (1) receiving psychoeducation about the nature of trauma and its impact, (2) learning to identify and process emotions, (3) engaging in self-disclosure, and (4) processing narrative development. The outcome of post-traumatic growth can include an increased appreciation of life; warmer, closer relationships with others; a greater sense of personal strength; recognition of new possibilities for one's life; and a greater appreciation of spirituality in life (Calhoun & Tedeschi, 2004). In the remainder of this chapter, we discuss how teachers can effectively respond to students in the aftermath of a crisis and promote recovery and post-traumatic growth. As we have noted, teachers are not therapists but can play an essential role in healing and recovery.

Responding in a Crisis

This section concerns both general and specific actions that teachers can take when responding to a crisis. In addition to general crises, we address the unique circumstances of the threat of suicide and the response to grief and loss. Finally, we return to the notion of developmental trauma and discuss the elements of trauma-sensitive practices.

Although teachers, like students, can be negatively affected by crisis events, they also can be models for students on how to cope with anxiety, fear, and stress after a crisis. Students, especially younger children, look to adults for clues about how to respond to an event. A teacher's calm presence can be reassuring to students and communicate that students are safe or, if not, what action needs to be taken next.

In addition to modeling calm behavior and reassuring students that they are safe, it is essential to limit students' exposure to the crisis event itself, especially frightening scenes of emergency medical treatment or those injured during a crisis (Brock et al., 2016). As we mentioned above, physical proximity to a crisis event increases the chances of trauma. In the same way, exposure to frightening images, including those of the media, after a crisis event also increases the risk of trauma. Recent research suggests that the more exposure to media information regarding the COVID-19 virus, the more anxious people are (Yao, 2020). Given this, adults should monitor and limit exposure to media images after a crisis (Brymer et al., 2012).

As discussed, social support from caregivers, caring adults, and peers can be an essential source of resilience when children face adversity (Masten, 2014). Teachers can be crucial sources of this social support during a crisis. One way to do so is to encourage students to interact more in class. For example, after a crisis event, teachers can increase group activities and collaborative assignments. Simply having students work together on academic projects can reduce stress and enhance a sense of safety and support (Brymer et al., 2012). Teachers can also directly address the importance of social support by discussing the importance of kindness and compassion after a crisis and by brainstorming with students the different ways to take action after a crisis, such as volunteering and becoming more active in addressing needs in their communities. Regaining the ability to actively (as opposed to passively) cope after a crisis is vital to recovery (Trickey et al., 2012). Finally, given the importance of social support, teachers can observe students who may seem withdrawn or isolated and need more attention or support.

Stabilization

Teachers also can help children to regulate the intense emotions that arise during and after a crisis. Masten (2014) describes how sensitive and competent adults help children manage their feelings and behaviors in a process that she calls *coregulation*. Teachers can play the role of coregulators with their students by modeling calm behavior, providing reassurance of safety, and, if needed, engage students in activities that stabilize them emotionally (Brymer et al., 2012).

When students are overwhelmed, the parts of their brain that problem solves, plans, or thinks things through have essentially gone "offline" (van der Kolk, 2014). Overwhelmed students may appear extremely agitated, panicked, or angry, which are all signs of hyperarousal. They may also feel numb, disoriented, or unresponsive, which would indicate dissociation. Given this, the goal of the teacher is to orient students to the present and help them to contain at least some of their emotional reactions. To do so, teachers must first have their own emotional reactions to the crisis under control.

For teachers to have a supportive conversation with students, the first step is to approach a student calmly and sit next to him or her. With some children or adolescents, a teacher can ask permission to place a "protective" arm around their shoulders. It is important always to ask permission and be sensitive to signs that physical contact may further overwhelm the student (Brock et al., 2016). The next step is to begin making psychological contact by saying the student's name (if you know it) and asking the student to look at you. For older students, teachers can ask basic information, such as their name, age, or grade. For younger children, it is appropriate to invite them to engage in neutral activities, such as drawing, coloring, or playing with favorite toys (Brock et al., 2016).

If these requests for basic information or the shifting attention to neutral activities do not sufficiently contain the students' distress and enable them to engage in a conversation, teachers also can use a grounding or stabilization strategy to further calm and orient students to the here and now. There are several valuable strategies, including asking the student to look around and describe the environment. The instructions for this can made more specific by asking students to name three things that they hear, two things that they see, and one thing that, through the sense of touch, they feel.

Another important stabilization strategy is to engage students in deep breathing. Simply breathing in through the nostrils for a slow count of four and breathing out for a count of four can reduce the fight or flight response and increase the activity of the parasympathetic nervous system, thus reducing anxiety and increasing feelings of calm. Teachers can combine deep breathing and activities by asking students first to take three slow deep breaths and then to look around the room to name three neutral things they see. Students can then take another three slow breaths and then name three sounds that they hear. Finally, after the third cycle of deep breaths, they can name three things that, through touch, they feel (Brymer et al., 2012).

As an example of how a teacher might use these strategies, we will turn to Sandy's scenario above. As noted, Sandy is 9 years old and in the fourth grade. She experienced the loss of her mother about a year ago and seemed to have had a strong reaction to the active shooter alert. She has been easily startled, irritable, and withdrawn since returning to school. You may remember that, when Sandy was told that she needed to go out and be with the other children during a break, she began to cry.

Teacher: "I am so sorry, Sandy. What is going on?"
Sandy: [Continues crying and does not respond.]
Teacher: "Sandy ... Sandy, can you please look at me." [Begins to orient Sandy to the present.]
Sandy: [Continues to cry but looks up at her teacher.]
Teacher: "Thanks ... there you go. Now, do me a favor and take a big, slow breath. We'll do it together. I will count as we breathe in and out. Ready?"
Sandy: [Nods and looks up a little more.]
Teacher: "Okay, let's go. One, two, three, four ... now breathe out. One, two, three, and four. That's great. We are going to do it two more times, okay?"
Sandy: [Sandy appears to participate as the teacher counts out the breathing two more times.]
Teacher: "Okay, that's really good, Sandy. Thanks. Now, we are going to do one more quick thing. Look around the room and tell me three things you see that you like." [By directing Sandy's attention to her senses, she becomes more present.]

Sandy:	"I see the cut-out flowers around the board over there. I see my table and chair, and I see my bag on the hook in the back."
Teacher:	"Great. Now tell me two things you hear. Nothing that makes you nervous, but just ordinary things."
Sandy:	"I hear Mrs. Jones talking outside and the birds outside the window."
Teacher:	"Okay, how about one thing you feel. I mean, like things you notice on your skin or in your muscles."
Sandy:	"I feel my legs on the chair."
Teacher:	"That is really good, Sandy, thanks. Now, take one more deep breath."
Sandy:	[Sandy takes another deep breath].
Teacher:	"Okay; can I ask you a couple of questions about what is going on now?"
Sandy:	"Okay."

As can be seen early in the dialogue, Sandy was not ready or even capable of talking about her reactions. The combination of deep breathing and using the 1-2-3 strategy to orient her to the here and now helped her to contain enough of her distress to appear to be ready to begin a conversation with the teacher. In the next section, we discuss the process of having this conversation and the strategies included in what is often called *psychological first aid* (PFA; Brymer et al., 2012).

Psychological First Aid

Like physical first aid, PFA seeks to stabilize someone and aids in beginning the process of healing. It is important to note that not everyone who experiences a crisis event will need PFA. Many students will either not have strong emotional reactions to a crisis or will recover using naturally occurring sources of social support (Brock et al., 2016). For those who have stronger responses to a crisis event, PFA can reduce distress and facilitate positive coping (Brymer et al., 2012).

Teacher-delivered PFA has grown out of a movement toward community-based PFA (Jacobs et al., 2016). Community-based PFA developed from the realization that it is difficult and often impossible to deploy enough trained mental health professionals to provide care to all those who need intervention after a crisis event. Training community members, including teachers, in PFA is a strategy to create a network of helpers who can listen supportively, understand reactions to crises, and know when and how to connect someone to professional assistance (Jacobs et al., 2016). It is also important to note that PFA is an immediate intervention that, although potentially helpful, is not psychotherapy and is not meant to resolve all of the problems that might arise from a crisis (Brock et al., 2016).

Different models for PFA exist, but all start with making psychological contact with students. Making contact may include introducing yourself, if you are not known to students, or, as in the situation discussed above, orienting students to the here and now and helping them to contain acute distress. As discussed above, making psychological contact for younger children also can include engaging them in emotionally neutral activities, such as drawing or playing with games or toys (Brock et al., 2016).

Another way to make contact and begin a conversation is to inquire about immediate needs and offer information about safety and the next steps in the crisis response. For example, a teacher may ask a student whether he is cold, thirsty, or hungry and then, if possible, provide a warm blanket or piece of clothing, water, or a snack. Teachers also should be equipped with sufficient information about a crisis incident to give necessary information to students. For example, a teacher might make a statement such as:

> What happened was super scary. I've been told that police and medical workers are making sure that we are safe and taking care of people who were hurt. We're all going to stay here for now until we get the message that it is okay to walk over to the grass at the end of the playground, where we'll meet your parents.

Basic information such as this reassures students and creates a sense of safety after a crisis event. Below is a dialogue between

Jose, a seventh-grade student, and his middle school history teacher, Mr. Allen, after an incident in which a man violated a restraining order by coming onto campus to confront his ex-wife, a popular lunchtime supervisor. They argued, and he hit her several times, until she was unconscious. She was taken to the hospital and is recovering. The police apprehended the perpetrator near campus within an hour of his fleeing. Jose was close to the victim. It is the next day, and Jose has his head down during most of the class. He lingers after class, and Mr. Allen asks him to sit down and then sits next to him.

Mr. Allen: "Hi, Jose. How are you doing since what happened to Mrs. Esparza yesterday? By the way, can I get you some water or a snack? I have some Power Bars in my desk" [Teacher asks about basic needs.]

Jose: "A Power Bar would be cool, thanks. I didn't eat breakfast today. I was too upset. She was always nice to me. It sucks that this happened."

Mr. Allen: "It sure does... It really sucks. You heard that she is in the hospital but doing okay. They say that she will recover and shouldn't have any long-term problems." [Reassuring information.]

Jose: "Oh, no, I didn't know that; that's good. What about the ex-husband, the dude who did it?"

Mr. Allen: "The police arrested him pretty fast, right after he ran away from the school. He didn't get very far, and I am pretty sure he is still in jail. The School Resource Officer is going to be here every day for a while, so people feel safe." [The teacher again provides information that is potentially reassuring.]

Mr. Allen: "That's good. Thanks for telling me."

The next step in PFA is listening and allowing students to explore their thoughts, feelings, and other reactions to the crisis. This is where the skills discussed in Chapter 5 come into play. As a reminder, these include minimal encouragers, paraphrasing and summarizing, conversational prompts, open-ended questions, and implied questions. In addition, scaling questions and relationship questions can be helpful tools when conducting PFA. Below, the conversation between Mr. Allen and Jose continues.

Mr. Allen:	"Jose, can I ask you another question?" [Asking permission to ask questions allows the student to retain a sense of agency in a situation in which they might feel little is under their control.]
Jose:	"Okay"
Teacher:	"Thanks. So, all this happened yesterday. What has it been like for you since you found out?"
Jose:	"I don't know… I was really upset. She was so nice. I don't understand why something like this happened to her."
Teacher:	"I know. It is always hard to figure out why something bad happens to someone nice. So, you were upset. Anything else?" [Expression of sympathy, short paraphrase, and open-ended question.]
Jose:	"I couldn't sleep last night… I kept thinking about her. It helps to know she is okay, though."
Teacher:	"I bet. It sucks that it happened but good to know she will be okay. Did you finally fall asleep? What did you do to help yourself fall asleep?" [Further expression of sympathy and another open-ended question.]
Jose:	"Yeah… I finally fell asleep… I don't know, maybe one [o'clock]. I played video games for a while, and then I remembered that breathing thing we learned in homeroom… You know, you breathe in slow and then breathe out for twice as long."

At this point in the conversation, Jose and his history teacher have begun to identify at least one specific problem related to the crisis incident: difficulty falling asleep. The steps presented below are meant to encourage Jose to engage in active coping. Encouraging active coping facilitates a sense of autonomy and self-efficacy that is important in recovering from a crisis. Jose has made this step easier by mentioning a strategy that he has used that he and his teacher can build upon to encourage further active coping.

Teacher:	"Oh, okay. That's great. Can you tell me a little more about this breathing thing?" [The teacher may or may not know about this strategy. Even if he does, it is helpful to have Jose explain it in his own words, thus reinforcing his knowledge of the strategy.]
Jose:	"You breathe… I don't know, maybe for four and then breathe out for eight. I guess the thing is to breathe out for longer than you breathe in."
Teacher:	"Okay, when you did it, how long did you do it for?"
Jose:	"I remembered about it late, and then I did it for … not sure … maybe two minutes."
Teacher:	"How'd it work? Think of it this way. On a scale of 1 to 10, 10 if it worked perfectly, and 1 is it didn't work at all, what number would you give it?" [Scaling question.]
Jose:	"Maybe a 7."
Teacher:	"Wow, that is pretty good. Sometimes if you do something like this for a little longer, it works even better. Let's try it together for … I don't know … maybe three minutes. What do you think?" [Jose's teacher reinforces Jose's use of the breathing strategy, and then he begins the process of exploring a small goal.]
Jose:	"Okay." [Jose and his teacher do the breathing strategy for three minutes.]
Teacher:	"How'd that work? What number would you give it now?" [Open-ended question and scaling question.]
Jose:	"An 8 or 9, I think."
Teacher:	"Okay, that's great. So, what do you think of trying that out for a couple of days and see if you feel better?" [Suggests small goal.]
Jose:	"Okay, sure."
Teacher:	"Great. So, Jose, if you don't feel better in a couple of days, I may want to see about you talking to a counselor. She may have some good ideas that I can't think of. Her name is Ms. Ruiz. Do you know

	who she is? [This brings the conversation to a close and prepares Jose for the possibility of a referral to a school-based mental health professional.]
Jose:	"I know her a little bit."
Teacher:	"Would it be okay if I ask her to talk with you if you are not sleeping better in a few days?"
Jose:	"That would be okay. I think I will feel better, though."
Teacher:	"I'm pretty sure that will be true. But just in case you need something more."
Jose:	"Okay."
Teacher:	"Cool. So, tomorrow, let's check in and see how things are going."
Jose:	"All right; after class, like now."
Teacher:	"Sure, that would be great. I'll see you tomorrow, then."
Jose:	"Okay, thanks. See you tomorrow."

To review, Jose and his history teacher have moved through a series of steps in the process of providing PFA. These steps include:

1. Making psychological contact.
2. Inquiring about basic needs.
3. Providing reassuring information about safety.
4. Asking about crisis experiences and actively listening.
5. Identifying specific crisis-related problems.
6. Problem solving and, if possible, setting a small goal.
7. Bringing the conversation to a close and explaining the next steps, including potential referrals to professional mental health providers.

One question in reading this dialogue is why Mr. Allen did not immediately refer Jose to a counselor, school psychologist, or another mental health professional. It is important to recall our previous statement that recovery is the norm. Making a referral for more intense and perhaps intrusive services can be harmful if not needed. Mr. Allen did two noteworthy things. He set the stage for a possible referral to the school counselor. Second, he communicated clearly that he would be looking for specific improvements in sleeping and would have Jose speak to the counselor if that did not improve. As we discussed in Chapter 1, teachers are uniquely positioned to observe students and notice if things are improving or worsening. In addition, by asking scaling questions, Mr. Allen has established a metric to judge progress. If, when next asked, Jose reports that he is still at 8 or perhaps has moved to 9, a referral to the school counselor may not be necessary.

Responding to Trauma: Trauma-Informed Practices

As discussed, most students who experience a crisis event will not develop enduring signs of trauma. Although resilience and recovery are the norm after a crisis event, many students will need longer-term support. In addition to those who suffer trauma due to an acute event, many students exhibit signs of trauma due not to a singular critical event but, instead, from chronic toxic stress. These students have often experienced the kinds of stressors discussed in Adverse Childhood Events (ACE) studies, including physical, sexual, and emotional abuse or neglect that arises from parental mental illness or substance abuse.

Whether the cause of the trauma is acute or long-term toxic stress, these students can exhibit symptoms of hyperarousal, dissociation, and intrusive thoughts. In addition, students whose ability to cope has been worn down over time by chronic stress are often mistrustful of adults and struggle to have supportive relationships with their peers (Jennings, 2019). A disruption in social relations is understandable, as nearly all of the stressors identified in the studies on exposure to adverse childhood experiences involve disruptions in the bond between children and their caretakers (e.g., abuse, neglect, absence of caregiver).

Research has shown that between a third and half of children have experienced at least one adverse childhood experience (Bucci et al., 2016). Exposure to ACEs and subsequent trauma is likely much worse in communities with fewer resources. In one study of an urban community in San Francisco, 67% of a community health clinic's patients had experienced at least one ACE (Burke et al., 2011). Given the number of children affected by trauma and its long-term consequences for learning and health, SAMHSA (2014) recommends that a range of supports be made available and that these services be provided in an "organizational or community context that is trauma-informed, that is, based on the knowledge and understanding of trauma and its far-reaching implications" (p. 2).

SAMHSA (2014) defines trauma-informed as including four assumptions: (1) a basic understanding of trauma and its impact, (2) the ability to recognize the signs of trauma, (3) the ability to respond using the principles of a trauma-informed approach at all levels of an organization, and (4) the resisting of practices that could inadvertently retraumatize. Earlier in this chapter, we provided an overview of trauma and its impact. In the remainder of this section, we focus on resisting practices that potentially retraumatize and how teachers respond to students who have signs of trauma.

Avoiding Retraumatization

Schools can unintentionally engage in practices that can be "triggering" or trauma-inducing for vulnerable students (Jennings, 2019; SAMHSA, 2014). These can include being punished, being faced with academic material that is too challenging or overwhelming, or being in an educational environment that is chaotic or unpredictable. Punishment is especially salient because many of the behaviors exhibited by traumatized students, such as inattention, irritability, and challenges with social relationships, can lead to coercive and exclusionary discipline.

There is strong evidence that these practices make things worse for students by further disconnecting them from teachers, peers, and school in general. Research has shown that zero-tolerance policies have led to many students being suspended or expelled with no evidence that these policies have made schools safer, which is their stated intent (American Psychological Association Zero Tolerance Task Force, 2008; Losen, 2014). Other research strongly links suspension and other exclusionary school discipline practices of the type that follow from zero-tolerance policies to a failure to graduate (Losen, 2014). Even more striking is the consistent racial and ethnic disparity in the frequency and severity of these types of exclusionary punishments in schools. For example, African Americans and students from other communities of color receive more frequent and harsher punishments than do white students for similar offenses (Skiba et al., 2002).

For these reasons, many schools are turning to restorative approaches to school discipline. There is no one agreed-upon definition of restorative justice or, more broadly, restorative practices, but different restorative approaches have several common elements. At the center of a restorative process is a focus on proactively creating community and positive relationships. This focus on relationships is carried into dealing with discipline and disruptive behavior, for which the goal is to maintain connections and relationships rather than exclude.

Restorative practices have been conceptualized as having two tiers (Green et al., 2018). Practices in the first tier include connection circles, whereby teachers lead classroom discussions that foster relationships, and restorative conversations, which are one-on-one conversations between a teacher and a student that lead to agreements about improving relationships. Second-tier practices focus on repairing relationships after someone's behavior has caused harm to the community of a classroom or school. Second-tier strategies include more formal problem-solving circles, restorative agreement meetings, and conflict mediation. Unlike exclusionary approaches to discipline, these strategies aim to repair the harm done to the relationship. Avoiding coercive discipline is critical for students who suffer from trauma. Restorative practices not only prevent the potential damage that comes from punishment but also take a proactive approach to promote relationships. This focus on relationships can be an essential factor in healing from trauma.

Responding from a Trauma-Informed Perspective

Returning to our discussion of the brain in Chapter 3, when we say that the fight-or-flight response is overactive, we are stating that the sympathetic nervous system is stuck in the "on" position and the *reptilian*, or older, part of our brain is in charge. Teachers can respond to students who suffer from trauma and help reduce the sympathetic nervous system's activation by creating a calm and predictable environment with predictable and easily understood routines, teaching self-calming and self-regulation strategies, and building safety through relationships. Many teachers already use strategies that establish helpful routines, such as opening and ending rituals (many of the circle strategies used in restorative practice create such rituals), playing calming music, or using visual schedules, to create a calm atmosphere in their classrooms and enhance the feeling of safety and engagement for the classroom.

Students also can be taught directly to calm the sympathetic nervous system by utilizing the breathing and stabilization strategies discussed above. These strategies include deep, slow breathing and learning to be present by noticing neutral things in the environment (e.g., "three things you see, three things you hear, and three things you feel"). A trauma-informed classroom utilizes these and other strategies, such as mindfulness (Jennings, 2019), as a regular part of the curriculum, resulting in the reduction of hyperarousal and dissociation.

For students, safety also arises from relationships or the activation of the limbic system of the brain. As discussed in Chapter 3, our brains are wired for connection, and supportive relationships are essential for self-regulation. In the context of a supportive relationship, students can be taught self-regulation strategies. To start, students need to learn a simple vocabulary for their feelings. Cross-cultural research on facial expressions suggests that there are only six basic human emotions. These include anger, disgust, fear, happiness, sadness, and surprise (Ekman, 1972). Although not a primary emotion, confusion or being mixed up is added to this list when teaching students a feeling vocabulary. The list of emotions then becomes sad, mad, glad, scared, surprised, bitter, and confused.

Naming emotions is the first step toward emotional self-regulation. The next step is to make judgments about the level or intensity of emotions. Students can learn to express these judgments through numbers (one to five or one to ten), colors (red, yellow, green), or the use of a graphic, such as a drawing of a thermometer.

In many ways, the practice of trauma-informed care is what caring teachers already do. They develop positive relationships in their classrooms and teach their students how to better cope with the stresses of their lives. Teachers who include social-emotional learning and restorative practices in their classrooms go a step further, not only in terms of accommodating their students' trauma but also by being an agent in their healing.

Healing Engagement: Cautions with a Trauma-informed Approach

Knowledge of the impact of trauma on students' lives is critical because it moves teachers and schools away from harsh discipline toward understanding that maladaptive behavior can be an expression of something deeper that is more important to respond to than what is on the surface. By focusing on students' trauma, we risk continuing to view these students and the communities they live in through a deficit lens. As we have discussed, the absence of psychopathology does not necessarily equal mental health. Ginwright (2018) proposes healing-centered engagement as an alternative framework. Healing-centered engagement acknowledges trauma but is also strengths-based. Importantly, it proposes that healing requires acknowledging that there are cultural, social, and political factors at work in creating the conditions that lead to exposure to trauma. As trauma specialist Resmaa Menakem states, "Trauma decontextualized in a person looks like personality. Trauma decontextualized in a family looks like family traits. Trauma in a people looks like culture." Being trauma-informed is important, and healing our students requires us to look beyond the suffering that follows trauma to the strengths and resources they have.

Conclusion

In this chapter, we have explained crisis and trauma and discussed typical responses to trauma. We have also reviewed ways that teachers can respond to students who are traumatized or have experienced a crisis. These responses include stabilization and Psychological First Aid. In addition to these strategies, we discussed the elements of trauma-informed teaching. In the next chapter, we discuss the threat of self-harm or suicide. Thoughts of self-harm are a unique type of crisis that can be both personal and communal. Although the danger of self-harm almost always requires the intervention of trained mental health professionals, teachers also have an essential role in recognizing suicidality and connecting students at risk for self-harm to the resources and services they need.

Takeaways

- With training, teachers can effectively provide care that mitigates some of the adverse consequences of crisis events.
- Trauma is the enduring adverse impact of a crisis. The sense of being overwhelmed that follows crises can lead to feelings of helplessness.
- There are two pathways to trauma. One is the result of acute crisis events, and the other arises with chronic stress or multiple prolonged stressful events in childhood.
- The enduring consequences of trauma include hyperarousal, intrusion, and dissociation.
- The steps to PFA include:
  - Making psychological contact
  - Inquiring about basic needs
  - Providing reassuring information about safety
  - Asking about crisis experiences and actively listening
  - Identifying specific crisis-related problems
  - Problem solving and, if possible, setting a small goal
  - Bringing the conversation to a close and explaining the next steps, including potential referrals to professional mental health providers
- Essential elements of a trauma informed approach include:
  - Understanding trauma and its impact on students
  - Avoiding practices that retraumatize

- Responding by creating calm and predictable environments, teaching self-calming strategies, teaching self-regulation strategies, and building safety through relationships

References

American Psychiatric Association. (2013). *Diagnostic and statistical manual of mental disorders* (5th ed.).

American Psychological Association Zero Tolerance Task Force. (2008). Are zero tolerance policies effective in the schools? An evidentiary review and recommendations. *The American Psychologist, 63*(9), 852–862.

Barenbaum, J., Ruchkin, V., & Schwab-Stone, M. (2004). The psychosocial aspects of children exposed to war: Practice and policy initiatives. *Journal of Child Psychology and Psychiatry, 45*, 41–62. https://doi.org/10.1046/j.0021-9630.2003.00304.x

Boxer, P., & Sloan-Power, E. (2013). Coping with violence: A comprehensive framework and implications for understanding resilience. *Trauma, Violence & Abuse, 14*(3), 209–221.

Brock, S. E., Nickerson, A. B., Louvar Reeves, M. A., Conolly, C. N., Jimerson, S. R., Pesce, R. C., & Lazzaro, B. R. (2016). *School crisis prevention and intervention: The PREPaRE model* (2nd ed.). National Association of School Psychologists.

Brock, S. E., Nickerson, A. B., Reeves, M. A., Jimerson, S. R., Liberman, R., & Feinbert, T. A. (2009). *School crisis prevention and intervention: The PREPaRE model.* National Association of School Psychologists.

Brymer, M., Taylor, M., Escudero, P., Jacobs, A., Kronenberg, M., Macy, R., Mock, L., Payne, L., Pynoos, R., & Vogel, J. (2012). *Psychological first aid for schools: Field operations guide* (2nd ed.). National Child Traumatic Stress Network.

Bucci, M., Marques, S. S., Oh, D., & Harris, N. B. (2016). Toxic stress in children and adolescents. *Advances in Pediatrics, 63*(1), 403–428. https://doi-org.libproxy.chapman.edu/10.1016/j.yapd.2016.04.002

Bufka, L. F., Wright, C. V., & Halfond, R. W. (2020). *Casebook to the APA Clinical Practice Guideline for the treatment of PTSD.* American Psychological Association.

Burke, N. J., Hellman, J. L., Scott, B. G., Weems, C. F., & Carrion, V. G. (2011). The impact of adverse childhood experiences on an urban pediatric population. *Child Abuse & Neglect*, *35*(6), 408–413. https://doi-org.libproxy.chapman.edu/10.1016/j.chiabu.2011.02.006

Calhoun, L. G., & Tedeschi, R. G. (2004). The foundations of posttraumatic growth: New considerations. *Psychological Inquiry*, *15*(1), 93–102.

Chafouleas, S. M., Johnson, A. H., Overstreet, S., & Santos, N. M. (2016). Toward a blueprint for trauma-informed service delivery in schools. *School Mental Health*, *1*, 144–162.

Cohen, J. A. (2010). Practice parameter for the assessment and treatment of children and adolescents with posttraumatic stress disorder. *Journal of the American Academy of Child & Adolescent Psychiatry*, *49*(4), 414–430. https://doi-org.libproxy.chapman.edu/10.1016/j.jaac.2009.12.020

Cook, A., Spinazzola, J., Ford, J., Lanktree, C., Blaustein, M., Cloitre, M., DeRosa, R., Hubbard, R., Kagan, R., & Liautaud, J. (2005). Complex trauma in children and adolescents. *Psychiatric Annals*, *5*, 390–398.

Ekman, P. (1972). Cross-cultural studies of facial expression. In P. Ekman (Ed.), *Darwin and facial expression: A century of research in review*. New York: Academic Press.

Felitti, V. J., Anda, R. F., Nordenberg, D., Williamson, D. F., Spitz, A. M., Edwards, V., Koss, M. P., & Marks, J. S. (1998). Relationship of childhood abuse and household dysfunction to many of the leading causes of death in adults. The adverse childhood experiences (ACEs) study. *American Journal of Preventive Medicine*, *14*(4), 245–258.

Gerson, R., & Rappaport, N. (2013). Traumatic stress and posttraumatic stress disorder in youth: Recent research findings on clinical impact, assessment, and treatment. *Journal of Adolescent Health*, *52*(2), 137–143.

Gilliland, B., & James, R. (1997). *Crisis intervention strategies*. Brooks/Cole.

Ginwright, S. (2018, May 31). The future of healing: Shifting from trauma informed care to healing centered engagement. *Medium*. https://ginwright.medium.com/the-future-of-healing-shifting-from-trauma-informed-care-to-healing-centered-engagement-634f557ce69c

Green, A. E., Willging, C. E., Zamarin, K., Dehaiman, L. M., & Ruiloba, P. (2018). Cultivating healing by implementing restorative practices for youth: Protocol for a cluster randomized trial. *International*

Journal of Educational Research. https://doi-org.libproxy.chapman. edu/10.1016/j.ijer.2018.11.005

Herman, J. (1992). *Trauma and recovery: The aftermath of violence from domestic abuse to political terror.* New York: Basic Books.

Jacobs, G. A., Gray, B. L., Erickson, S. E., Gonzalez, E. D., & Quevillon, R. P. (2016). Disaster mental health and community-based psychological first aid: Concepts and education/training. *Journal of Clinical Psychology, 72*(12), 1307–1317. https://doi-org.libproxy.chapman. edu/10.1002/jclp.22316

Jennings, P. A. (2019). Teaching in a trauma-sensitive classroom: What educators can do to support students. *American Educator, 43*(2), 12–17.

Kessler, R., Sonnega, A., Bromet, E., Hughes, M., & Nelson, C. (1995). Posttraumatic stress disorder in the National Comorbidity Survey. *Archives of General Psychiatry, 52*(12), 1048–1060

Losen, D. (Ed.). (2014). *Closing the school discipline gap: Equitable remedies for excessive exclusion (disability, equity and culture).* Teachers College Press.

Lowe, S. R., & Galea, S. (2017). The mental health consequences of mass shootings. *Trauma, Violence, & Abuse, 18*(1), 62–82. https://doi-org. libproxy.chapman.edu/10.1177/1524838015591572

Masten, A. S. (2014). *Ordinary magic: Resilience in development.* Guilford Press.

McCabe, O. L., Everly, G. S., Brown, L. M., Wendelboe, A. M., Abd Hamid, N. H., Tallchief, V. L., & Links, J. M. (2014). *Psychological first aid: A consensus-derived, empirically supported, competency-based training model.* https://doi-org.libproxy.chapman.edu/10.2105/ AJPH.2013.301219

McNally, R. J., Bryant, R. A., & Ehlers, A. (2003). Does early psychological intervention promote recovery from post-traumatic stress? *Psychological Sciences in the Public Interest, 4,* 45–80. https://doi. org/10.1111/1529-1006.01421

Michael, T., Ehlers, A., Halligan, S. L., & Clark, D. M. (2005). Unwanted memories of assault: What intrusion characteristics are associated with PTSD? *Behaviour Research and Therapy, 43*(5), 613–628.

National Institute of Mental Health. (n.d.). *Helping children and adolescents cope with disasters and other traumatic events: What parents, rescue* workers, and the community can do. Government Printing Office. https://www.nimh.nih.gov/health/publications/helping-children-and-adolescents-cope-with-disasters-and-other-traumatic-events/index.shtml

National Institute of Mental Health. (2002). *Mental health and mass violence: Evidence-based early psychological intervention for victims/survivors of mass violence. A workshop to reach consensus on best practices.* Government Printing Office. http://www.nimh.nih.gov/research/massviolence.pdf

Ratcliffe, M., Ruddell, M., & Smith, B. (2014). What is a "sense of foreshortened future?" A phenomenological study of trauma, trust, and time. *Frontiers in Psychology, 5,* 1026.

Skiba, R. J., Michael, R. S., Nardo, A. C., & Paterson, R. L. (2002). The color of discipline: Sources of racial and gender disproportionality in school punishment. *The Urban Review, 34*(4), 317–342.

Slaikeu, K. A. (1990). *Crisis intervention: A handbook for practice and research* (2nd ed.). Allyn & Bacon.

Substance Abuse and Mental Health Services Administration. (2014). *SAMHSA's concept of trauma and guidance for a trauma-informed approach* (HHS Publication No. 14-4884). http://store.samhsa.gov/shin/content/SMA14-4884/SMA14-4884.pdf

Tedeschi, R. G. (2020). Growth after trauma: Five steps for coming out of a crisis stronger. *Harvard Business Review, 98*(4), 127–131.

Tedeschi, R. G., & Moore, B. A. (2016). *The posttraumatic growth workbook: Coming through trauma wiser, stronger, and more resilient.* New Harbinger Publications.

Trickey, D., Siddaway, A. P., Meiser-Stedman, R., Serpell, L., & Field, A. P. (2012). A meta-analysis of risk factors for post-traumatic stress disorder in children and adolescents. *Clinical Psychology Review, 32*(2), 122–138. https://doi-org.libproxy.chapman.edu/10.1016/j.cpr.2011.12.001

van der Kolk, B. (2014). *The body keeps the score: Brain, mind, and body in the healing of trauma.* Viking.

Yao, H. (2020). The more exposure to media information about COVID-19, the more distressed you will feel. Brain, Behavior, and Immunity, 87, 167–169.

7

Responding to the Threat of Suicide

Suicide is a large and growing public health problem in the United States. Notably, it is the second leading cause of death among youth 10–14 years old and adolescents and young adults aged 15–24 (Hedegaard et al., 2020). The number of youth suicides also appears to be increasing at an alarming rate. For example, for youth aged 15–19, the rate of suicide increased by 76% between 2007 and 2017 (Curtin & Heron, 2019).

Completed suicide is the final step in a sequence of experiences that include thinking about suicide, making plans, and acting on those plans (Miller, 2011). Data from a nationwide survey of risk behaviors (Kann et al., 2016) found that almost 18% of adolescents in the United States reported seriously considering suicide, close to 15% reported making plans to kill themselves, and nearly 9% had attempted suicide one or more times. These data mean that, at any given moment in a high school with 2,000 students, over 350 students could be thinking of suicide, nearly 300 are not only thinking about it but are making specific plans, and about 170 have tried to kill themselves.

The risk of suicide varies among different groups of adolescents. For example, males are almost twice as likely to die from suicide, even though females are nearly twice as likely to think about suicide or make plans to end their lives

DOI: 10.4324/9780367810269-7

(Centers for Disease Control and Prevention, 2016). Although males are more likely to die from suicide, recent data suggest that the gender gap in lethality has decreased as girls and young women choose more lethal means to commit suicide (Ruch et al., 2019).

Suicide rates are also higher in rural communities than in urban areas for both males and females (Pettrone & Curtin, 2020). In some ways, this finding runs counter to the stereotype that urban environments are more stressful and isolating. Yet, many rural communities have limited access to health care in general and mental health care specifically. This gap in access to services that might treat mental health issues that often underlie suicide or intervene when the threat of suicide arises plays a significant role in the higher rates of suicide found in rural areas of the United States.

Lesbian, gay, bisexual, transgender, and questioning or queer youth (LGBTQ+) are also at greater risk of suicide. LGBTQ+ adolescents are nearly four times more likely than heterosexual youth to attempt suicide or be injured in a suicide attempt (Centers for Disease Control and Prevention, 2017). Transgender youth are four to five times more likely to attempt suicide than are their peers who exclusively identify as their sex assigned at birth (i.e., cisgender) (Johns et al., 2019).

Teachers and Suicide

Early identification of students at risk is a critical step in reducing suicide (Torok et al., 2019). Although students who consider suicide need professional mental health services, the magnitude of the problem suggests that there is unlikely to be enough trained mental health professionals to identify and assist all those in need. Given this, the Substance Abuse and Mental Health Services Administration (2012) and the National Strategy for Suicide Prevention (Office of the Surgeon General and the National Action Alliance for Suicide Prevention, 2012) recommend that all adults in school communities be trained to identify and respond to at-risk students. As with community-based psychological first aid (PFA; Jacobs et al., 2016), involving the entire school community rather than only mental health professionals in suicide prevention is more likely to identify students in need and prevent suicide. Among those in the school community, the National Strategy for Suicide Prevention regards teachers as "key gatekeepers" and emphasizes teachers' role in suicide prevention (Office of the Surgeon General and the National Action Alliance for Suicide Prevention, 2012).

Research supports the importance of teachers' role in suicide prevention and has found that it is common for students to approach teachers regarding suicidality. In a survey of high school teachers, 75% of the teachers knew at least one student who had attempted or died by suicide (Westefeld et al., 2007). In another study of high school teachers (Freedenthal & Breslin, 2010), 20% of teachers had spoken directly with at least one student who shared suicidal thoughts or behavior during the prior year.

Therefore, it is not surprising that teachers view themselves as having a role in suicide prevention. In yet another study of high school teachers (Hatton et al., 2017), all but one of the 74 teachers surveyed agreed that they should play a role in suicide prevention. However, in this same study, only a third of the participants indicated that they made themselves available to talk with students about personal issues. The perceived barriers to engaging more with suicidal students included limited training, fears of making the situation worse, and legal repercussions. However, those who had prior training in suicide prevention were twice as likely to have a student approach them to talk about suicide. Students, of course, probably did not know that these teachers were trained. Instead, these teachers likely exhibited in subtle ways a greater openness.

Training can also address teachers' perceived barriers, such as believing that they will make things worse or be exposed to legal liability. Training could reduce these concerns, particularly the inclusion of data that no teacher or school system has been sued for making good-faith efforts to prevent suicide. Instead, notably, schools have faced legal consequences for failure to notify parents, obtain assistance for a student at risk of suicide, or adequately supervise a student at risk of suicide (Juhnke et al., 2011; Lieberman et al., 2006). The notion that talking about suicide will make things worse is, of course, a myth. In fact, talking to someone about suicide is a critical way to reduce suicidality.

As we noted above, a community approach to suicide prevention and intervention views teachers as gatekeepers. This concept is very similar to the notion of "gateway providers," discussed in Chapters 2 and 4. As with mental health challenges, in general, effective gatekeepers (1) understand the high prevalence of suicide, (2) know the risk factors and warning signs associated with suicide, (3) have the skills to respond to suicide risk, and (4) know how to connect students to professional help.

Risk Factors and Warning Signs

When mental health professionals assess suicide risk, they consider risk and protective factors and, most importantly, immediate warning signs (Hass, 2018). Warning signs are immediate indications that someone desires to die and has the capacity to act on that desire. Risk factors are characteristics of persons, families, or social or historical factors that research on suicide has shown increases a person's vulnerability over time and include the demographic variables noted above, such as being male, living in a rural area, and being LGBTQ+. Other important risk factors include mental illness, prior suicide attempts, and substance or alcohol abuse. Risk factors such as these can co-occur and build on one another, thus increasing overall risk (Shaffer et al., 1996).

The primary difference between warning signs and risk factors is that risk factors are the background and do not, by themselves, indicate immediate risk. Instead, risk factors suggest where schools and communities can focus their prevention efforts to mitigate the risk of suicide. In contrast, warning signs are behaviors or verbal expressions that indicate an acute threat in the immediate moment. Although mental health professionals' comprehensive suicide assessments can focus on both risk factors and warning signs, teachers who serve as gatekeepers will focus on warning signs.

Warning signs consist of observable behaviors and statements made by a student that indicate an increased desire to die and a growing capacity to act on this desire (Van Orden et al., 2010). These might include talking or writing about death, dying, or suicide; direct threats to kill oneself; making plans or looking for ways to kill oneself; and taking action to obtain the means to kill oneself (American Association of Suicidology, n.d.). This progression from talking or writing about suicide to actively seeking the means to kill oneself is on a continuum from less to more risk. Speaking or writing about death, dying, or suicide indicates suicidal ideation or thinking about suicide. Direct threats to kill oneself suggest a greater desire to die, while making specific plans or seeking means represents not only a desire to die but a growing capacity to act.

Warning signs of suicide

- Talking or writing about death, dying, or suicide
- Making plans to kill oneself
- Taking action to obtain the means to kill oneself

It is also vital to understand protective factors related to suicide. With suicide, as with mental health challenges and stress in general, the most potent protective factor is social support. This finding again highlights the importance of purposefully developing positive relationships in the classroom, as discussed in Chapter 3. Social support also has been identified as a buffer against several of the important risk factors associated with suicide, including depression (Skärsäter et al., 2005; Underwood, 2000) and substance abuse (Acri et al., 2012; Richter et al., 1991).

Skills for Suicide Prevention

Even if teachers understand the prevalence of suicide and have knowledge of risk factors and warning signs, they also need specific skills to respond effectively to students at risk of suicide (Hatton et al., 2017). The communication skills required to intervene when there is a risk of suicide include the listening skills discussed in Chapter 5. A helpful first step is the strategy of *breathe, look, and remind*, discussed in Chapter 5. When beginning a conversation with a student who is considering suicide, it is crucial to take a deep breath and bring yourself into the moment. Students who are thinking of killing themselves can be deeply distressed, and it is critical that you, the listener, be as calm as possible. For the last step, *remind,* it is also essential for teachers to remind themselves that, even with suicide, a teacher's job is not to solve the underlying problems that bring a student to consider killing him or herself. Instead, a teacher's task is to listen supportively, ask specific questions that help estimate risk, and connect the student to the appropriate resources.

It is also vital that teachers who interact with youth at risk of suicide be aware of their beliefs and attitudes about death and suicide and how they may affect their ability to be supportive (Miller, 2011). For example, although perhaps well intended, it is not helpful to make statements such as, "You have so much to live for. Why would you consider killing yourself?" or "Have you thought of how much this would impact those you leave behind?" Instead, teachers must listen carefully to what students say about their experiences and try to understand how they came to consider ending their lives.

Below is a dialogue between Julie, a 13-year-old eighth-grade student, and her Language Arts teacher, Ms. Alvarez. Ms. Alvarez had given the class an assignment to discuss their future and how they may differ from the 19th-century characters in the books that they had read recently. Julie's essay had struck Ms. Alvarez as dark. She was apprehensive about a comment that Julie had written: "I don't see much of a future for myself. In fact, I don't see myself in the future. Ms. Alvarez invited Julie to come by during the lunch break to talk with her.

Ms. Alvarez: "Hi, Julie; thanks for meeting with me. I wanted to ask you about the essay you recently turned in. I was worried when you wrote that you didn't see much

	of a future for yourself. I was surprised because … I don't know … I see a pretty bright future for you. You're smart and work hard. You could do a lot of things."
Julie:	"I don't know. You know there is so much going on, and I feel stressed all the time."
Ms. Alvarez:	"Oh, that sounds tough. What is going on that you feel stressed all the time?" [Expression of sympathy, open question that echoes Julie's words.]
Julie:	"I work so hard, but I am never going to get into a good school for college, and my friends suck. They don't care about school and think I am no fun because I don't feel like doing anything. I should study, but most of the time, I don't feel like it. My parents just tell me not to worry so much, but what do they know?"
Ms. Alvarez:	"Okay, wow, a lot is going on. Let me see if I get it. You are worried that you won't get into a good college even if you work really hard, your friends think you are no fun, and your parents don't get you. Is that about it?" [Summary statement.]
Julie:	"Yeah, I just don't see how things are going to change."
Ms. Alvarez:	"I see. Can we go back to your essay, and can I ask you a couple of questions about it?" [Asking permission to direct the conversation in a different direction.]
Julie:	"Okay, I guess."
Ms. Alvarez:	"What did you mean when you wrote, 'In fact, I don't see myself in the future?'" [Ms. Alvarez transitions the conversation to the specific behavior that led to her concern.]
Julie:	"I don't know. What is the use of going on if nothing is going to work out?"

Here the teacher begins a shift from just listening and exploring Julie's concerns to asking specific questions to screen for suicide risk. The questions asked to assess the immediate threat of suicide can vary in their wording but typically follow the continuum of risk discussed above and consist of questions that focus on significant immediate warning signs. These include suicidal ideation—thinking of suicide, making plans to carry out suicide, and taking action to initiate these plans.

Different versions of these questions exist. For example, the Columbia-Suicide Severity Rating Scale (C-SSRS; Posner, 2007; Scott et al., 2004; Shaffer et al., 2004) is one of the most researched suicide screening tools available (Carter et al., 2019). Versions of the C-SSRS have been developed for use in schools (The Columbia Lighthouse Project, n.d.) and the military and healthcare workers and emergency responders. Table 7.1 below presents the kinds of questions teachers can ask to screen students for the risk of suicide. The questions will be exemplified as Ms. Alvarez, and Julie's conversation continues.

The dialogue above ended with Julie saying, "I don't know. What is the use of going on if nothing is going to work out?" As

TABLE 7.1 Risk Assessment Questions

Sample Questions	Domain of Risk
1. Have you ever thought about killing yourself or wished you were dead?	Question regarding suicidal ideation
2. How often do you think about killing yourself? Every day? Once in a while?	Questions to further explore suicidal ideation
3. How long have you been having these thoughts?	
4. Have you considered acting on those thoughts?	Initial questions regarding plans
5. Have you considered doing something rather than just thinking about it?	
6. Have you been thinking about how you might do this?	
7. Do you have a plan?	Questions to further explore plans
8. Have you worked out the details of how you might kill yourself?	
9. Do you mean to carry out this plan?	
10. Do you have access to _____? (gun, poison, rope)	
11. Have you ever tried to hurt yourself before?	Actions taken
12. Have you ever started to act on your plan but stopped?	

the conversation continues, Ms. Alvarez asks Julie questions to estimate Julie's immediate risk for suicide.

Ms. Alvarez: "Julie, sorry, I have to ask you this. Have you been thinking about killing yourself? [Notice the directness of this question. When discussing suicide with a student, it is crucial to be as unambiguous as possible.]

Julie: [Julie looks down and away and seems to tear up.]

Ms. Alvarez: "It is okay. I know this is hard to talk about, but I want to make sure you are safe. So, have you been thinking of hurting yourself?" [Expression of sympathy and support and then repeating the question.]

Julie: "I don't know; I guess so, sometimes. Nothing seems worth living for anymore."

Ms. Alvarez: "I am sorry that things are so bad for you. Do you think about it a lot?" [Another expression of sympathy and support followed by a question about the frequency of the suicidal thoughts.]

Julie: "Not all the time; maybe a couple of times a week."

Ms. Alvarez: "Okay, have you thought about how you might kill yourself? Any plans?" [Question about plans.]

Julie: "No, not really."

Ms. Alvarez: "Okay. Are you sure? No ideas about how you might do it?" [Follow-up question about plans.]

Julie: "Yeah, every time I begin to think about how I would do it, it just seems so terrible, I stop thinking about it."

Ms. Alvarez: "Okay, Julie. I am glad you told me about all this. You are very brave. Let's talk about what we are going to do."

A first step in connecting students to help is to know the policies and legal issues related to suicide. These are different from state to state, and school districts within a state will vary in implementing the state's policies and legal mandates. In the United States, 25 states mandate suicide prevention training, while 14 encourage staff training (Hatton et al., 2017). An example of a comprehensive statewide suicide policy for schools is found in California's Assembly Bill No. 2246. Passed in 2016, AB 2246 states:

> The governing board or body of a local educational agency that serves pupils in grades 7 to 12, inclusive, shall, before the beginning of the 2017–18 school year, adopt, at a regularly scheduled meeting, a policy on pupil suicide prevention in grades 7 to 12, inclusive. The policy shall be developed in consultation with school and community stakeholders, school-employed mental health professionals, and suicide prevention experts and shall, at a minimum, address procedures relating to suicide prevention, intervention, and postvention.

AB 2246 also stipulates that the policy adopted should address the needs of high-risk groups, such as youth bereaved by suicide; youth with disabilities, mental illness, or substance use disorders; youth who experience homelessness or live in out-of-home settings, such as foster care; and LGBTQ+ youth. Finally, it mandates that teachers be trained in suicide awareness and prevention. We advocate that all teachers should become aware of policies and laws in their jurisdiction. Further, if training is not mandated, teachers should seek out and advocate for training in suicide awareness and prevention. In addition, no matter the policy or legal mandates in a particular state, teachers need to be aware of community resources, such as suicide hotlines.

Ms. Alvarez should be aware that she cannot agree to keep what Julie has shared with her a secret and that she should not leave Julie alone. In screening for suicide risk, answering "yes" to any of the risk assessment questions, including occasionally thinking about suicide, requires connecting the student to a mental health provider. Although students such as Julie do not appear to present an immediate or acute risk—she is thinking about suicide but does not have specific plans—Ms. Alvarez will need to contact one of the school's mental health providers as soon as possible and, if needed, walk with Julie to the campus counseling office.

In some cases, there may not be a mental health professional available. For example, a teacher or coach may have a conversation with a student after school, or the school's mental health provider may not be on campus. Schools should have procedures for a situation such as this. For example, Ms. Alvarez could, after explaining the situation, leave Julie with a school administrator who will stay with Julie until her parents pick her up. In cases in which even this option is not available, Ms. Alvarez may need to contact Julie's parents directly and wait with her until she is picked up or call the local mental health emergency hotline. Below, the conversation continues:

Ms. Alvarez: "Julie, I am sorry, but when someone tells me that they are thinking of hurting themselves, I have to tell someone else. So, what I would like to do is to call Mrs. Anderson, the school psychologist, and then walk with you down to her office." [It is essential to state clearly that you must inform someone. Also note that Ms. Alvarez is being direct and telling Julie what they are going to do.]

Julie: "Do you have to tell? Will you tell my parents? I don't want them to know. They will just get freaked out."

Ms. Alvarez: "I think, in the end, Mrs. Anderson will decide that, but probably she will want to talk with your parents. She'll help them understand and not get freaked out. Don't worry. As I said, you are very brave, but I don't think you can deal with this by yourself, and I can't be the only person trying to help you. I know Mrs. Anderson, and she will definitely be super supportive and help you figure this all out."

Julie: "Okay, I am just so embarrassed."

Ms. Alvarez: "I understand, Julie. The important thing is we are going to get you some help so you can get past this."

Julie: "Okay."

Ms. Alvarez: "Wait just a minute while I call the counseling office and tell them we are coming up. [Ms. Alvarez calls the office and tells Mrs. Anderson that she and Julie

	are on the way.] Got your stuff? Okay, let's go. It is going to be all right." [Reassurance.]
Julie:	[Julie picks up her bag, and she and Ms. Alvarez begin to walk to the office.]

There are many "what ifs" involved in connecting Julie to help. In one of the studies of high school teachers mentioned above (Westefeld et al., 2007), 67% of the teachers surveyed were not aware of their high school's procedures for intervening with a suicidal student. Given this, an essential first step is for teachers to be informed of the practices schools have established regarding the threat of suicide. As we have discussed, if the conversation with Julie had occurred after school, or a mental health professional such as Mrs. Anderson was not available, Ms. Alvarez would then have to decide whether it was best to (1) take Julie to a school administrator and, together, contact Julie's parents or guardians to pick her up; (2) if an administrator was not available, to try to contact Julie's parents herself; or (3) if the parents or other emergency contact were not available, to call the local mental health emergency hotline. In some communities, there is a crisis team or psychiatric emergency team that, if called, will come to the school to do a comprehensive evaluation and, if needed, arrange for in-patient psychiatric care.

Conclusion

Suicide is a critical public health problem, and teachers have an essential role in its prevention. As with mental health problems, students spend so much time in school that teachers are well-positioned to recognize the signs of suicide. Most importantly, by knowing the signs of potential suicide and having the skills to screen for risk, teachers can play a critical role in identifying students at risk for suicide and connect them to the help they need. In the next chapter, we expand our discussion of creating connections between students and school and community resources. We also focus on the importance of investigating district-based and other local resources designed to support children and their families. We then discuss how teachers can serve as a bridge between students, families, and these resource providers.

Takeaways

- Suicidal behavior, including thinking of suicide, planning suicide, and making attempts to commit suicide, are common, especially among adolescents and young adults.
- Although males are more likely to die by suicide, females are more likely to consider killing themselves.
- LGBTQ+ adolescents are nearly four times more likely than are heterosexual youth to attempt suicide or be injured in a suicide attempt.
- Warning signs of suicide include

    - Talking or writing about death, dying, or suicide.
    - Making plans to kill oneself.
    - Taking action to obtain the means to kill oneself.

- Social support is a powerful buffer against suicide and the mental health problems that often precede thoughts of killing oneself.
- Teachers can play an essential role in preventing suicide.

References

Acri, M. C., Gogel, L. P., Pollock, M., & Wisdom, J. P. (2012). What adolescents need to prevent relapse after treatment for substance abuse: A comparison of youth, parent, and staff perspectives. *Journal of Child & Adolescent Substance Abuse, 21*(2), 117–129.

American Association of Suicidology. (n.d.). *Know the warning signs of suicide*. http://www.suicidology.org/resources/warning-signs

Carter, T., Walker, G. M., Aubeeluck, A., & Manning, J. C. (2019). Assessment tools of immediate risk of self-harm and suicide in children and young people: A scoping review. *Journal of Child*

Health Care, *23*(2), 178–199. https://doi-org.libproxy.chapman.edu/10.1177/1367493518787925

Centers for Disease Control and Prevention. (2016). *Fatal injury reports*. [Injury Prevention & Control: Data & Statistics (WISQARSTM)]. https://www.cdc.gov/injury/wisqars/fatal_injury_reports.html

Centers for Disease Control and Prevention. (2017). *Youth risk behavior survey—Data summary & trends report: 2007–2017*. https://www.cdc.gov/healthyyouth/data/yrbs/pdf/trendsreport.pdf.

Curtin, S. C., & Heron, M. (2019). *Death rates due to suicide and homicide among persons aged 10–24: United States, 2000–2017* (NCHS Data Brief, No. 352). National Center for Health Statistics.

Freedenthal, S., & Breslin, L. (2010). High school teachers' experiences with suicidal students: A descriptive study. *Journal of Loss & Trauma*, *15*(2), 83–92. https://doi-org.libproxy.chapman.edu/10.1080/15325020902928625

Hass, M. (2018). *Interviewing for assessment: A practical guide for school counselors and school psychologists*. John Wiley & Sons.

Hatton, V., Heath, M. A., Gibb, G. S., Coyne, S., Hudnall, G., & Bledsoe, C. (2017). Secondary teachers' perceptions of their role in suicide prevention and intervention. *School Mental Health: A Multidisciplinary Research and Practice Journal*, *9*(1), 97–116. https://doi-org.libproxy.chapman.edu/10.1007/s12310-015-9173-9

Hedegaard, H., Curtin, S. C., & Warner, M. (2020). *Increase in suicide mortality in the United States, 1999–2018* (NCHS Data Brief, No. 362). National Center for Health Statistics.

Jacobs, G. A., Gray, B. L., Erickson, S. E., Gonzalez, E. D., & Quevillon, R. P. (2016). Disaster mental health and community-based psychological first aid: Concepts and education/training. *Journal of Clinical Psychology*, *72*(12), 1307–1317. https://doi-org.libproxy.chapman.edu/10.1002/jclp.22316

Johns, M. M., Lowry, R., Andrzejewski, J., Barrios, L. C., Demissie, Z., McManus, T., Rasberry, C. N., Robin, L., & Underwood, J. M. (2019). Transgender identity and experiences of violence victimization, substance use, suicide risk, and sexual risk behaviors among high school students—19 states and large urban school districts, 2017. *Morbidity and Mortality Weekly Report*, *68*(3), 67–71.

Juhnke, G. A., Granello, D. H., & Granello, P. F. (2011). *Suicide, self-injury, and violence in the schools: Assessment, prevention, and intervention strategies*. John Wiley & Sons.

Kann, L., McManus, T., Harris, W. A., Shanklin, S. L., Flint, K. H., Hawkins, J., Queen, B., Lowry, R., O'Malley Olsen, E., Chyen, D., Whittle, L., Thornton, J., Lim, C., Yamakawa, Y., Brener, N., & Zaza, S. (2016). Youth risk behavior surveillance—United States, 2015. *Morbidity and Mortality Weekly Report*, 65(6), 1–174. https://www.cdc.gov/healthyyouth/data/yrbs/pdf/2015/ss6506_updated.pdf

Lieberman, R., Poland, S., & Cowan, K. (2006). Suicide Prevention in the Schools. *Principal Leadership*, 7(2), 11–15.

Miller, D. N. (2011). *Child and adolescent suicidal behavior: School-based prevention, assessment, and intervention*. Guilford Press.

Office of the Surgeon General and the National Action Alliance for Suicide Prevention. (2012). *National strategy for suicide prevention: Goals and objectives for action: A report of the U.S. Surgeon general and of the National Action Alliance for Suicide Prevention*. U.S. Department of Health & Human Services. https://www.ncbi.nlm.nih.gov/books/NBK109917/

Pettrone, K., & Curtin, S. C. (2020). *Urban-rural differences in suicide rates, by sex and three leading methods: United States, 2000–2018* (NCHS Data Brief, No. 373). National Center for Health Statistics.

Posner, K. (2007). Columbia-Suicide Severity Rating Scale. *PsycTESTS*. https://doi-org.libproxy.chapman.edu/10.1037/t52667-000

Richter, S. S., Brown, S. A., & Mott, M. A. (1991). The impact of social support and self-esteem on adolescent substance abuse treatment outcome. *Journal of Substance Abuse*, 3(4), 371–385. https://doi.org/10.1016/S0899-3289(10)80019-7

Ruch, D. A., Sheftall, A. H., Schlagbaum, P., Rausch, J., Campo, J. V., & Bridge, J. A. (2019). *Trends in suicide among youth aged 10 to 19 years in the United States, 1975 to 2016. JAMA Network Open*, 2(5). https://doi-org.libproxy.chapman.edu/10.1001/jamanetworkopen.2019.3886

Shaffer, D., Gould, M. S., Fisher, P., Trautman, P., Moreau, D., Kleinman, M., & Flory, M. (1996). Psychiatric diagnosis in child and adolescent suicide. *Archives of General Psychiatry*, 53(4), 339–348. https://doi.org/10.1001/archpsyc.1996.01830040075012

Shaffer, D., Scott, M., Wilcox, H., Maslow, C., Hicks, R., Lucas, C. P., Garfinkel, R., & Greenwald, S. (2004). The Columbia suicide screen: Validity and reliability of a screen for youth suicide and depression. *Journal of the American Academy of Child and Adolescent Psychiatry*, 43(1), 71–79.

Skärsäter, I., Langius, A., Ågren, H., Häggström, L., & Dencker, K. (2005). Sense of coherence and social support in relation to recovery in first-episode patients with major depression: A one-year prospective study. *International Journal of Mental Health Nursing, 14*(4), 258–264. https://doi.org/10.1111/j.1440-0979.2005.00390.x

Substance Abuse and Mental Health Services Administration. (2012). *Preventing suicide: A toolkit for high schools.* https://store.samhsa.gov/shin/content//SMA12-4669/SMA12-4669.pdf

The Columbia Lighthouse Project. (n.d.). *Empowering schools, campuses & communities to prevent suicide & violence with the Columbia Protocol (C-SSRS): A vital component of school safety & community protection.* https://cssrs.columbia.edu/

Torok, M., Calear, A. L., Smart, A., Nicolopoulos, A., & Wong, Q. (2019). Preventing adolescent suicide: A systematic review of the effectiveness and change mechanisms of suicide prevention gatekeeping training programs for teachers and parents. *Journal of Adolescence, 73*, 100–112. https://doi-org.libproxy.chapman.edu/10.1016/j.adolescence.2019.04.005

Underwood, P. W. (2000). Social support. The promise and the reality. In V. H. Rice (Ed.), *Handbook of stress, coping, and health. Implications for nursing research, theory, and practice* (pp. 367–391). Sage.

Van Orden, K. A., Witte, T. K., Cukrowicz, K. C., Braithwaite, S. R., Selby, E. A., & Joiner, T. J. (2010). The interpersonal theory of suicide. *Psychological Review, 117*(2), 575–600. https://doi.org/10.1037/a0018697

Westefeld, J. S., Kettmann, J. D. J., Lovmo, C., & Hey, C. (2007). High school suicide: Knowledge and opinions of teachers. *Journal of Loss and Trauma, 12*, 33–44.

8

Beyond Instruction

Connecting Students and Families to Resources

At the end of every student teaching experience, the state of California requires that teacher candidates create a document called the Individualized Development Plan (IDP). In this document, candidates set goals and objectives for their first two years of full-time teaching, during which they are paired with a mentor who assists them in meeting their aims to earn their preliminary teaching credentials.

After student teaching in a high school setting during the COVID-19 pandemic, a time fraught with multiple student mental health crises and professional isolation, one teacher candidate declared the following rationale for an objective on her IDP:

> Another experience limited by the pandemic was my ability to interact and work with other members of the high school community. Although I was able to meet the principal, one of the vice principals, a few of the office members, as well as a few of the other 10th grade English teachers, there were never many opportunities for collaboration. I am able to work well independently (and I had the support and guidance of my mentor teacher) but going forward I would

like to hear a variety of ideas and strategies. I know I still have a lot to learn about teaching, and I know I can rely on other educators to help me grow in my practice.

Importantly, when this student teacher came to the section on the form where she needed to list specific strategies, she noted that her intention was to meet with several on-campus specialists, such as school psychologists, school counselors, speech and language pathologists, and special education teachers, "so [she] can better support [her] students and become a part of the community." She also noted a desire to "explore the neighborhood the school is in as well as the neighborhoods that feed into the school." This teacher candidate's awareness that she needs to be more knowledgeable about resources available for her students and be part of a support team, rather than trying to meet students' needs alone, provides the perfect starting point for this chapter. In the following sections, we focus on how teachers can connect students and families to academic, social, health-related, and other support services that contribute to their healing and well-being (Ginwright, 2016).

As we have discussed, no student or classroom exists in isolation. Thus, it is critical that teachers actively foster relationships between their classrooms—the microsystem in Brofenbrenner's ecological model—and the surrounding systems of their schools, school districts, families, and communities. It is easy to imagine how students and families might benefit from these networks. Nurturing these connections is also an issue of practicality and self-preservation for teachers, as teachers need to be equipped to plan, teach, assess, and reflect to support students' academic needs. Although teachers are increasingly aware of the importance of supporting students' socioemotional needs, there could come a time when a student or family requires more than a teacher, even one knowledgeable and skilled in mental health, can provide. In such case, teachers need to know that they can remain in their role as teachers and help students to get what they need. Learning about district and community resources, establishing relationships with those in charge, and knowing how to effectively connect students and families to such resources can take the pressure off teachers who may feel overwhelmed by their students' needs and their sense of duty to serve families well.

Because teachers are often cheered as the people who will *change the world*, it is important to remember that they are already doing quite a bit of good simply by implementing high-quality pedagogical practices. Welcoming and valuing students and families, creating a caring classroom community that uses mindfulness practices, and designing lessons that are culturally responsive and culturally sustaining are all important. Notably, cultivating students' curiosity and awareness about the world, while simultaneously developing academic skills, habits, talents, and potential, are critical to changing the world for the better. Finally, reflecting continuously on their practice, paying particular attention to their own implicit biases, goes a long way toward meaningfully supporting students' socioemotional and academic development. Others' acknowledgment that teachers' work, on its own, contributes to student and family mental health is a critical component of counteracting the burnout that many teachers face (discussed further in Chapter 9). Based on our own experience as parents, just our knowing that there is another thoughtful adult available to assist with our children's healthy development eases the burden of parenting while also enhancing its joy.

There are times, however, when a student, family, or community's needs are so great that a caring and intellectually engaging classroom is not enough. In addition, a family may need support not often available at school, such as access to a healthcare clinic (although even health clinics are sometimes available on school campuses). As we noted in our discussion of resilience, children access multiple sources of support as they develop. Having these sources, which include individuals, groups, or agencies, effectively relate to one another can have a powerful effect, particularly in cases where poverty and systemic injustices are prevalent. Although there are multiple ways to forge connections, share resources, and reciprocate expertise, what is available in school and in the community to students and families in times of need needs to be clarified. Teachers do not have to be social workers or psychologists to be good at their jobs, even if they might feel that way sometimes. They just have to know people who have professional expertise and engage them proactively when help is needed.

Getting to Know the School System You Work In

It can be easy to forget that there are often multiple specialists and programs present to support teachers' work and the needs of students and families. One of the problems with the way that these resources are organized in schools is that they often are not well coordinated with one another and, thus, operate in relative isolation. Teachers need to create a resource map as a way to identify existing resources and specific personnel that a teacher may draw upon to support students and families. Developed by the Center for Mental Health in Schools at the University of California, Los Angeles (http://smhp.psych.ucla.edu/), resource maps can take various forms. The version below, which we use with our teacher and school psychology candidates and was adapted from resource maps on the Center's website, focuses on the identification of people, roles, and responsibilities.

An added benefit of getting to know student support service providers is that teachers have someone with whom to share stories about particular students when they are at a loss for what to do next. In these conversations, they can get their questions answered and help to generate ideas for what other support services might be needed at the school site. Being in community in this way supports teachers and benefits students.

Although the map above contains a list of critical personnel who may perform specific roles in students' lives, a district or school also might have particular programs that target students' academic, social, or health needs. For example, at one school Amy taught at, the school psychologist set up a weekly open-ended play session for primary grade students who were struggling with making friends at school. Students referred by their teachers would attend the weekly group, learning to interact with other children with intentional adult guidance as they played with blocks or pretended using

TABLE 8.1 Adapted from School/District Personnel Resource Map: Critical Personnel

Key Support Staff: School/District	Roles and Responsibilities	Contact Information and Times at School
School Psychologist: [name]	Providing student mental health services, testing, advising in regard to supporting specific students in the classroom, attending IEP meetings, and coordinating school-based mental health response both proactively and when there is a crisis in the community or at school.	[email address, phone]; Mondays and Wednesdays, 7:30 am–3:30 pm
School Nurse: [name]	Providing health screenings, medication distribution, and health education programs for students and families and CPR trainings for faculty and staff.	[email address, phone]; Tuesdays and Wednesdays, 7:30 am–3:30 pm
School Safety Officer: [name]	Greeting students and families at drop off and pick up, receiving deliveries, signing in visitors and volunteers to the school, securing the campus, and coordinating safety trainings for faculty and staff.	[email address, phone]; Monday–Friday, 7:00 am–4:00 pm
Student Attendance Review Board (SARB)/Attendance Counselor/dropout prevention: [name(s)]	Tracking and recordkeeping related to student attendance, serving on SARB, and connecting families to community resources that will support attendance, behavior, and dropout prevention.	[email address, phone]; Monday–Friday, 7:30 am–3:30 pm
Social Worker: [name]	Serving as student and/or family caseworker, connecting families to community resources, and participating in Student Study Team meetings.	[email address, phone]; Mondays, noon–3:30 pm
School Counselor: [name]	Working with students who are struggling with behavior or personal issues, advising, and/or taking the lead on schoolwide programs connected to academic success and socioemotional health.	[email address, phone]; Tuesdays and Thursdays, 7:30 am–3:30 pm
Community Liaison: [name]	Talking with families or students in need, connecting families to community resources, conducting home visits on behalf of the school, providing translation for written communication, and interpreting support for school meetings and parent-teacher conferences.	[email address, phone]; Monday–Friday, 8:00 am–noon

(Continued)

TABLE 8.1 Adapted from School/District Personnel Resource Map: Critical Personnel *(Continued)*

Key Support Staff: School/ District	Roles and Responsibilities	Contact Information and Times at School
Bilingual/ELD support: [name]	Conducting testing of individual students to assess their knowledge of English and running small instructional groups in English Language Development.	[email address, phone]; Monday–Wednesday, 7:30 am–3:30 pm
Speech and Language Pathologist: [name(s)]	Providing speech and language support for students who receive services as per their Individualized Educational Plan.	[email address, phone]; Thursdays, 7:30 am–3:30 pm
Resource and Special Education Teacher(s): [name(s)]	Serving on student study teams, writing Individualized Education Plan (IEP) goals, providing specialized instruction to students with IEPs, assessing student IEP goal progress, and co-teaching with general education teachers.	[email address, phone]; Monday–Friday, 7:30 am–3:30 pm
Library and Media Specialist: [name)]	Running the school library in all aspects: ordering books and media resources, facilitating checkout systems and record keeping, supporting instruction with media literacy lessons, and assisting teachers in locating resources for units of study.	[email address, phone]; Monday–Friday, 7:30 am–3:30 pm
School-based Crisis Team (list by name/title)	Principal: [name] Assistant Principal: [name] Administrative Assistant: [name] School Safety Officer: [name] School Psychologist: [name] School Counselor: [name] School Nurse: [name] Lead Teacher(s): [name(s)]	Meets first Monday of the month, 3–4 pm
School-based Student Study Team (list by name and title)	Administrator: [name] School Psychologist: [name] Resource Specialist: [name] Occupational Therapist: [name] Speech and Language Pathologist: [name]	Meets every Tuesday, 1–2 pm

puppets. This same school, which followed a community school model (Oakes & Espinoza, 2020), had a health clinic on campus so that when a student had a toothache, they could be walked across the playground to see a dentist right away. Schools might also offer academic support through programs such as Advancement Via

Individual Determination (AVID) or provide counseling during times of community crisis. Knowing what is available is an essential first step in making an eventual referral. One way to document these program resources could look like this:

TABLE 8.2 Adapted from School/District Program Resource Map: Support Programs

	Academic Support	
Name of Program	*Description of Program*	*Person In-charge and Contact Information*
Gifted and Talented Education (GATE)	Offers academic enrichment activities to students who test into the program.	[name of GATE director, email address, phone number]
Reading Recovery	Offers one-on-one instruction to struggling first grade readers.	[name of Reading Recovery specialist, email address, phone number]
English Language Development (ELD) Support	Offers small group instruction by an ELD specialist.	[name of ELD specialist, email address, phone number]
	Behavioral Support	
Lunch with the Principal	Yard duty and teachers are given slips of paper to record specific incidents of students' being caught in the act of "being good." Students receive the slip from their teacher or a yard duty staff and put it into a jar in the office. Five slips a week are pulled, and winners receive a special pizza lunch with the principal.	All teachers and yard duty staff work in collaboration with the school office.
Peer-led Conflict Resolution	A team of upper grade students is trained in conflict resolution by the school counselor; they are available at recess to help students resolve minor playground disputes.	[name of School Counselor, email address, phone number]
Restorative Justice	A student accountability program dedicated to repairing harm done to the community by a student's behavior.	[name of Restorative Justice school site leader, email address, phone number]

(Continued)

TABLE 8.2 Adapted from School/District Program Resource Map: Support Programs *(Continued)*

Mental Health Support

Name of Program	Description of Program	Person In-charge and Contact Information
Mindfulness Program	School psychologist leads teachers and students in a six-week mindfulness training.	[name of School Psychologist, email address, phone]
Support group for families dealing with childhood cancer	School psychologist leads weekly support group for parents whose children have cancer.	[name of School Psychologist, email address, phone]
School-based mental health services	Onsite mental health services for students and families in crisis.	[name of School Psychologist, email address, phone]

Physical Health Support

Name of Program	Description of Program	Person In-charge and Contact Information
Morning Running Program	Physical Education teachers supervise students who run around the school track one hour before school begins, Monday through Friday.	[P.E. teachers' names, email addresses, phone]
School Soccer Team	School soccer team comprised of third to fifth grade students; practices on Monday through Friday after school, one game per week during fall semester.	[Name of faculty coach, email address, phone]
Mobile Dentist Program	University-sponsored mobile dentist conducts oral hygiene education program for Kindergarten through second grade classrooms.	[Name of Mobile Dentist Program Director, email address, phone]

Other Student Programs

Name of Program	Description of Program	Person In-charge and Contact Information
Family Ambassador Program	Family Ambassadors have families of kindergarteners or other new families to the school over to their house for a meal to welcome them to the school community.	[PTA Family Ambassador Chair's name, email address, phone number]
Knitting Club	Teacher-led after-school program in which students learn to knit together.	[Teacher-leader's name, email address, phone number]
Folklorico Dance Group	Teacher-led after-school dance program focused on learning and performing Folklorico dances from Mexico.	[Teacher-leader's name, email address, phone number]

Resource mapping (Adelman & Taylor, 2006) aims to clarify the resources available, who facilitates the service, and how the service works. Such knowledge is essential, as the teachers, along with other school personnel who support the same children and families, are subject to the same pressure to serve these constituents effectively. Creating these maps is the first step in understanding how services are coordinated and how to leverage them efficiently. These maps also could be used to uncover gaps that need to be addressed.

Because these services are not always well known at a school, teachers will often need to talk to multiple people at their school sites and within their school district to complete a resource map. Notably, job title terminology could vary. For example, a district near where we work has positions called "school counselor," "school psychologist," "student support specialist," and "wellness specialist." Each of these positions plays a role in providing mental health support, but the specifics of the support services that they provide are often not evident from their titles. Thus, teachers need to seek out this information and develop a resource map every time they enter a new school and at the beginning of any new school year, as staffing or programs might change. Whenever possible, teachers should introduce themselves to these specialists so that a relationship can be formed. Being proactive in mapping resources and building associated relationships is especially helpful when a crisis arises and help is needed urgently.

Reflection

Create a plan to develop a resource map for your school or district, based on the examples above. What additional roles need to be added to the chart, given your specific school or district context? What roles need to be clarified? How can you go about seeking out that information?

General Roles of School Support Personnel

It may be the case that, as a teacher, you have heard a particular job title but are not sure what role that position fills in a school or district. Below are some generic job descriptions of key, non-instructional personnel informed by what is listed on the California Teachers Association (2021) website (https://www.cta.org/for-educators/meet-cta/student-support-services). Keep in mind that specific responsibilities may vary from state to state or district to district, depending on local needs.

School Nurses: School nurses are registered nurses (RNs) with a health services credential. Their responsibilities might include health screenings, medical referrals, health education, staff health-related professional development, first aid, child abuse reporting, school-based wellness initiatives, and basic student health care (e.g., managing students' medicine at school). According to the National Association of School Nurses (2016), they are responsible for upholding Standards of Practice as they coordinate care, provide health-related leadership, ensure the quality of care, and facilitate public health as they support students and families.

School Psychologists: School psychologists also have state-issued credentials and are trained in education and psychology specifically. They are specialists in mental health. Their responsibilities might include leading schoolwide mental health initiatives and professional development, assessing students and assisting with special education services connected to Individualized Education Plans (IEP), and helping teachers to create positive classroom environments and learn strategies to support individual students. According to the National Association of School Psychologists (2021), school psychologists play a vital role in ensuring academic achievement for a diverse group of learners while promoting healthy student behavior and psychological wellness that results in a positive school climate overall. By engaging families and coordinating services, school psychologists assist in short-term and long-term solutions for students and schools in need.

School Librarians: School librarians are credentialed teachers who also have a Library Media credential. They manage the school library as well as support students' literacy development. Their responsibilities might include working with classroom teachers on locating informational or text resources, teaching information literacy skills and helping students to locate books they might enjoy, and caring for and curating the physical and digital library within the school. According to the American Association of School Librarians (2021), school librarians are also responsible for students' media literacy skills, facilitating technological access to information, and encouraging students to use critical thinking skills as they consider the sources of information they are using to learn.

School Counselors: School counselors are also credentialed to provide academic advising, career counseling, and personal counseling. They work with others in the school community to support students in a variety of ways. Their responsibilities might include offering counseling to students regarding academic planning and emotional support, coordinating with community partners to support students' academic and social development, and creating policies to support school attendance and other initiatives that work toward student success. According to the American School Counselor Association (2021), school counselors help students' short- and long-term goals and provide school site leadership in fostering equity and access for all students through data analysis and advocacy.

> **School Social Workers:** School social workers have a master's degree in social work and are credentialed by the state. Their role is to support families and students in school. Their responsibilities might include student and family case management; developing intervention strategies; facilitating dialogue between the family, community, and the school; and playing a role in a student study team. According to the School Social Work Association of America (2021), a school social worker connects the home, school, and community as they support students by working to cultivate and meet IEP goals and making referrals to outside agencies. The National Association of Social Workers (2021) states that school social workers also can facilitate school discipline policies and crisis management.

Connecting Families to the Wider School System and the Community

When thinking about student mental health, it is important to keep in mind that building relationships between the school and community offers additional possibilities. Resource maps of youth and family services both within and beyond the school district context can be helpful tools for teachers to share with families. Knowledge of school lunch program offerings, parks and recreation opportunities, nonprofit services, school district collaborations with outside agencies (e.g., Boys and Girls Club, YMCA), and summer enrichment programs can be as important as knowledge of how to access low-cost medical providers, counseling services, food pantries, and child care providers. Having relationships with outside service providers enables teachers to be community conduits.

One example of the effectiveness of this type of networking comes from a research study that I (Amy) did on the identification of literacy-related resources for children who are living without permanent housing (MacGillivray et al., 2010). An interview with one school administrator whose school served a significant population of precariously housed elementary students provided insight into what an intentional effort to support children and families might look like. Immediately upon enrollment, families and school officials had intake meetings. These gatherings provided the administration with critical information about which resources the family had access to and what was still needed with respect to students' academic, social, and emotional needs. These gatherings also helped to initiate a relationship of caring between the family and the school. Because the school was well networked in the community, personnel could put families in touch with a variety of services, including providing children's eye exams, locating school supplies, and securing scholarships to local summer camps and enrichment programs. Notably, the school had made a concerted effort to reach out to local government officials, nonprofits, universities, and charities to develop collaborative relationships. As a result, when new services became available, these community organizations would call the school to determine whether they had a student or family who could benefit. These relationships helped school personnel to respond quickly to families when a need arose.

The school's reputation in the community was bolstered not just by a firm commitment to serve its constituency but also through its state recognition for academic excellence. Because this school's leader leveraged strong relationships in the school and the community, she could promise her families, teachers, staff, and students that she would do whatever it took to ensure their individual and collective success. Further, this allowed teachers a space to focus on academic endeavors.

Because it might be inefficient for individual teachers to reach out to every community organization on their own, creating a resource map, such as the one below, might be better left to other school personnel. Once completed, instructional leaders would be wise to invite district and community support providers to staff and faculty meetings to develop a schoolwide shared understanding about what is available and who the ideal candidates for each service are. Providing links on the school website or even having a simple binder or

TABLE 8.3 Adapted from Neighborhood and Community Program Resource Map

After-school Programs

Name of Program	Description of Program	Person in Charge and Contact information
Homework Club	The school library is open from after school until 5 pm Monday through Thursday so that students can complete their homework.	[Librarian's name, email address, phone]
Open Playground	The school playground is open for free play after school until 5 pm Monday through Friday.	[Head Yard Duty staff's name, email address, phone]
Boys and Girls Club	Boys and Girls Club employee picks students up after school and takes them to their Center; open until 7:00 pm Monday through Friday.	[Boys and Girls Club Director's name, email address, phone]; program web address

Academic Enrichment Programs

University Writing Project	Local university students facilitate 10-week writing project in fall and spring every Wednesday, 3:00–3:45 pm.	[School Faculty Liaison's name, email address, phone]
Public Library Read Aloud Program	Children's librarian reads aloud to local K–3 students every Saturday, 9–10 am.	[Children's Librarian at local public library's name, email address, phone]; program web address
Summer STEM Program	Local nonprofit offers a summer program for K–8 students interested in STEM.	[Nonprofit Director's name, email address, phone]; program web address

Town/City/County Recreational Programs

Swimming Lessons	Public swimming pool offers swimming lessons, water safety classes, and junior lifeguard training for K–12 students, May through September.	[Public Pool Director's name, email address, phone]; program web address
Children's Community Theater Program	Children's Community Theater puts on four musicals a year with a cast of K–12 students.	[Children's Community Theater Director's name, email address, phone]; program web address
Nonprofit Spring Break and Summer Day Camp Programs	Local nonprofit provides day camp programs for K–8 students during spring break and summer, Monday through Friday, 9:00 am–3:00 pm.	[Nonprofit Director's name, email address, phone]; program web address

(Continued)

TABLE 8.3 Adapted from Neighborhood and Community Program Resource Map *(Continued)*

	Other Programs Available to Families	
Name of Program	Description of Program	Person in Charge and Contact information
Local Food Pantry	Offers free food to families in need.	[Nonprofit organization's name, email address, phone number]; website information
Parenting Classes	Local nonprofit offers parenting classes for parents of infants, toddlers, and elementary school age children, four sessions per year.	[Nonprofit organization's name, email address, phone number]; website information
Nonprofit Mental Health Service	Local nonprofit assists uninsured families with mental health services.	[Nonprofit organization's name, email address, phone number]; website information

bulletin board in the school office that includes information, flyers, business cards, or brochures can make for a more efficient process of connecting families to outside agencies when they need help.

Acting As an Ambassador among Support Providers, Students, and Families

Once critical needs and the appropriate resources are identified, teachers need to facilitate sustained relationships by fostering introductions and following up on whether support is being provided. Simple actions, such as walking a student to the school psychologist's office and introducing them to each other, can play an essential role in ensuring that a student connects with the appropriate professional. It also sends a message that the support person is an ally. Further, following up with both parties without asking for specific details provides a measure of accountability.

For community resources, it is worthwhile to call the agency ahead of time to ensure that a referral is appropriate. It is important to keep in mind that, for many families, the logistics of connecting to a community resource are challenging. It is helpful for teachers to know what accessing help at a particular agency looks like for students or parents. For example, who answers the phone? Is there an intake interview? It also may be beneficial to discuss other practical issues, such as transportation or insurance. Once this information is clear, and after connecting with the family to make sure that they would like to engage with a particular resource, teachers could offer further support by helping to complete an online application for the family or visiting the agency together. Follow-up by a professional is critical, and it is vital to not simply give families a name and phone number and expect that they will be able to make the connection independently.

Although a teacher could offer the help discussed above, in many cases, the logistics of this level of assistance to connect families to community resources may be too much of a burden. Teachers may not have all the information that they need, or they may not have correct information because they are hearing about a need indirectly. In these cases, assistance might be better left to a colleague who has more expertise or a different kind of relationship with a family. In these situations, it is essential to work with other personnel, such as administrators, school psychologists, school counselors, or school social workers, to help families to connect to community resources. Here is a sample dialogue between a teacher and the principal about a student that demonstrates what this type of conversation might look like:

Teacher: "Hi, Mrs. Galloway. Do you have a minute?"
Principal: "Sure, come on in."
Teacher: "I think I mentioned to you that one of my students, Ricky, has been acting very needy lately. It's been okay, just a little strange, like he wants to stay in the classroom with me instead of going to the yard at recess. It's fine. I give him a job to do, and he seems content chatting about his favorite TV shows as he passes out papers or sharpens pencils for me. Since

he has not been direct with me about what might be happening, I introduced him to our school counselor so that they could begin a relationship. I know they have met once. Anyway, his friend Hunter's dad came by the classroom after school today to let me know that Ricky has been eating dinner at their house every night this week. When this dad drives Ricky home after dinner, sometimes the mom is not yet home from work, so he brings Ricky back to their house to spend the night. Can you help me to figure out what to do?"

Principal: "Thanks for letting me know about this. I am aware that this family is having some difficulties. I'm glad to know that Ricky is meeting with the school counselor and that you are offering him a safe space for him to be in the classroom when he needs it. As far as connecting Ricky's family to some community resources, we are already working on that, so be assured that I will take it from here. Please let me know if anything changes with Ricky's behavior, if he mentions something you find to be a Child Protective Services concern, or you hear more from Hunter's dad."

Teacher: "I will. Thanks."

Among other things, this conversation again highlights the power of relationships. By offering what the principal calls a "safe space," the teacher is providing a powerful intervention. Further, although not mentioned in the conversation, Hunter's dad is also providing support. Ricky's situation is complicated. Although he may struggle with what is happening with his family (the details are not yet known to the teacher), the ultimate target of the community resources the principal mentions, will be the entire family.

Helping families to make connections to community resources can be a powerful act of solidarity. Nevertheless, teachers need to be aware of the power dynamics at play. They should not coerce families into services that they do not want or that might put them at risk (as might be the case with undocumented families). It might be difficult for a family to refuse a teacher's suggestion, especially if the teacher is someone whom they want to please due to their role in the child's life. At the same time, a teacher's endorsement of a particular community program might help to motivate a family to take advantage of an opportunity. Using professional judgment is crucial here, as the ethics might be tricky, depending on the context or circumstances. Before taking action, soliciting a trusted colleague's or administrator's advice is necessary to have another perspective on what might go wrong or be inappropriate.

Of course, connecting a family to a community resource will be easier if teachers and the families have worked together to support students from the first day of school. The relationship-building strategies mentioned earlier, such as calling families to introduce themselves, emailing or writing with good news about a student's accomplishments, or stopping a family at school drop-off to provide a compliment about their child's behavior, grow trust. Then, when a family needs help, they already view the teacher as the kind of person capable of assisting, as the teacher already has established themselves as someone who has their child's best interests at heart. Below is a sample dialogue between a parent and a teacher in regard to a community resource. This dialogue assumes that a relationship of goodwill has already been established and that the teacher remains respectful of a family's right to make its own decisions for their child.

Teacher: "In our last parent-teacher conference, we discussed how much Juan loves to read. It would be great for him to continue his interest in books over the summer."

Parent: "Yes. He loves to read."

Teacher: "The local public library has a summer reading program that you can enroll Juan in. If he reads ten books or more, he can earn two free movie tickets. Does that sound like something that you might want for him? Or something that he might be interested in?"

Parent: "Yes, but we will be in Mexico all summer visiting family, so I am not sure that he will be able to

	participate. But the book club would be a good idea, since he always gets so sad when he is away from his friends for the summer. We are always looking for activities to cheer him up when we are there."
Teacher:	"I thought that it might be the case that you would be away, so I called the librarian to see what alternatives might exist. She mentioned that, with his library card, Juan can check out books electronically. Does he have a library card?"
Parent:	"No, not yet."
Teacher:	"You can get one over the internet free of charge. Would you like me to help fill this out with you?" [Uses the classroom computer to locate the public library website.]
Parent:	"That would be great." [They fill out the form, with the parent's asking questions of the teacher when they arise.]
Teacher:	"So glad this is working out. Will Juan have access to an iPad and internet in Mexico?"
Parent:	"Internet, yes, but we do not have an iPad."
Teacher:	"Let me talk to the technology people at the school district to see if he can check one out over the summer break. If that works out, I can show Juan how to enroll in the summer reading challenge when I share the opportunity with the class next week. If he does, maybe a way to help with his homesickness would be to have him talk about books with other students in the class who will also be participating in the reading program. The students can meet online to discuss the books after they read them. That might help Juan feel connected to his peers even when he is out of town. How does that sound?"
Parent:	"Wonderful. Thank you."

Although, in this case, the parent was agreeable to the plan, it would have also been fine if the parent had not. All teachers can do is offer to connect the family to the resource. Even if the parent decided to turn an opportunity down, the parent learned that the teacher wanted to encourage Juan to read and talk about books with his peers over the summer. The parent also learned that the teacher was willing and prepared to help make that happen.

> **Reflection**
>
> Think about when a student or family who needed resources that you could not provide as part of classroom learning. How did you handle that situation? How does the information from this chapter so far inform that incident as you look back on it? What might you do differently moving forward?

Why Should Schools Serve in These Capacities?

Earlier in this chapter, we referred to two reasons that families and students might need support that goes beyond the institution of school: healing and well-being. Ginwright (2016) defines healing as what is necessary to obtain a baseline level of physical and mental health in the midst of trauma. Well-being is what is required to thrive. This distinction echoes our early discussions about a dual-factor model of mental health, resilience, and posttraumatic growth. The processes of recovery and growth that Ginwright describes as healing and thriving are often co-occurring.

Ginwright (2016) notes that, in many communities, particularly ones populated predominantly by people of color and low-income families, the harm to the individual is often connected to unjust systems of economic oppression and systemic racism. Addressing the individual and societal needs simultaneously is required if circumstances are to improve. To do so requires collective action, which is why it is so important that schools be involved with facilitating relationships between families and support services while being part of the overall societal solution. For this reason, informing a family about a summer reading program that their child might enjoy, and that offers an opportunity to be in a community with others to talk about those books, takes on greater meaning. Not only does the specific program bolster student literacy development over the summer break, but a teacher's initiative to connect the family with the public library and facilitate a related social connection sends an important message to the family that the teacher is an ally in cultivating their child's intellectual development, joy, sense of kinship, and accomplishment.

When thinking back to the school principal who chose to see the potential of her precariously housed students, it is clear that she not only ensured that families had their basic survival needs met but also inspired her faculty and staff to do everything they could to foster students' growth so that they could thrive. In this way, Ginwright's (2016) notion of transformative organizing, which moves us to rethink how we relate to one another individually and institutionally, can be powerful. Taking time to listen deeply to families; reflect on the political, historical, and cultural nature of schooling; and think about how the nature of schooling affects particular choices and actions in supporting students' healing and well-being can help to guide teachers ethically in their decision making. Transformative organizing also may inform educators about developing a better notion of the future that we want to create within and between schools and other institutions. Because these issues are complex and context specific, it is critical that teachers are reflective in their approach in terms of which resources to identify as potentially supportive and how best to facilitate a relationship between families and service providers.

Reflection

- What cultural, linguistic, or social factors might be at play in your specific school or district context? Given these factors, what do families say are their pressing needs?
- What ways can you think of to connect students and families to school, district, and community resources?
- What implicit or explicit biases of your own might be at play in your expectations of families, their needs, and how they might respond to attempts to connect them to resources? How might you mitigate them?

Takeaways

- Many high-quality pedagogical practices meaningfully support students' social-emotional and academic development. Yet, it is important for teachers to coordinate with other service providers, as their classrooms do not sit in isolation.
- Resource mapping (Adelman & Taylor, 2006) helps to identify existing resources and specific personnel that a teacher may draw upon to support students and families. Maps can help to identify key personnel within a school or district as well as programs that support the academic, social-emotional, and physical well-being of students.
- Resource maps also can be made to identify critical community services that include those that support students' academic and social development as well as those organizations and programs that support the overall health and well-being of families, such as health clinics, food pantries, and legal support services.
- After a relationship of trust and caring has been established with families, teachers can serve as important ambassadors for these resources.
- Teachers should be mindful that addressing individual needs and related societal injustice simultaneously is required for students and families to heal and thrive. Being reflective and making ethical decisions is key to being a part of positive collective action. Engaging with colleagues to check in on any implicit biases or potential negative consequences will support teachers in doing right by students and families.

References

Adelman, H., & Taylor, L. (2006). Mapping a school's resources to improve their use in preventing and ameliorating problems. In C. Franklin, M. B. Harris, & P. Allen-Meares (Eds.), *The school services sourcebook: A guide for social workers, counselors, and mental health professionals* (pp. 977–990). Oxford University Press.

American Association of School Librarians. (2021, July). *Learning about the job*. https://www.ala.org/aasl/about/ed/recruit/learn

American School Counselor Association. (2021, July). *The role of the school counselor*. https://www.schoolcounselor.org/getmedia/ee8b2e1b-d021-4575-982c-c84402cb2cd2/Role-Statement.pdf

California Teachers Association. (2021, June). *Student support services*. https://www.cta.org/for-educators/meet-cta/student-support-services

Center for Mental Health in Schools at UCLA. (2015). Resource mapping and management to address barriers to learning: An intervention for systemic change. http://smhp.psych.ucla.edu/pdfdocs/resourcemapping/resourcemappingandmanagement.pdf

Ginwright, S. (2016). *Hope and healing in urban education: How urban activists and teachers are reclaiming matters of the heart*. Routledge.

MacGillivray, L., Ardell, A. L., & Curwen, M. S. (2010). Supporting the literacy development of children living in homeless shelters. *The Reading Teacher, 63*(5), 384–392. https://doi.org/10.1598/RT.63.5.4

National Association of School Nurses. (2016). Framework for 21st century school nursing practice: National Association of School Nurses. *NASN School Nurse, 31*(1), 45–53. https://doi.org/10.1177/1942602X15618644

National Association of School Psychologists. (2021, July). *Who are school psychologists*. https://www.nasponline.org/about-school-psychology/who-are-school-psychologists

National Association of Social Workers. (2021, July). *School social work*. https://www.socialworkers.org/Practice/School-Social-Work

Oakes, J., & Espinoza, D. (2020). *Community schools the New Mexico way*. Learning Policy Institute.

School Social Work Association of America. (2021, July). *School social work as a career*. https://www.sswaa.org/ssw-career

9

Teacher Self-Care, Self-Compassion, and Self-Renewal

Every year, the master's degree graduation ceremony for our teacher education candidates is a day filled with hope. During this ceremony and its immediate aftermath, there is an unshakable feeling that the world is going to be a better place. This energy comes from a collective witnessing of smart, caring, reflective, and committed people who are celebrating their investment in themselves. The members of the graduating class are exhilarated to enter our classrooms as teachers, a role they consider to be their spiritual and intellectual calling. The audience cheers loudly, grateful for what this group has accomplished and for the profound impact that these educators will have on our collective future.

Squaring this experience with the statistics on teacher burnout is, therefore, difficult. Of new teachers, 44% leave the profession within five years, with teachers of color leaving at proportionally higher rates than their white colleagues (Ingersoll et al., 2018). This high turnover is inherently destabilizing to students, families, schools, communities, and society, especially in rural and urban communities that experience poverty. For this reason, teacher stress and mental health must receive collective focused attention, as it is an issue that affects more than just teachers.

DOI: 10.4324/9780367810269-9

Teacher Mental Health as an Ethical Need

What happens between graduation and that day when teachers decide that they cannot continue to sustain themselves in their chosen career? Notably, teaching is considered one of the most stressful professions (Busby, 2019). This is due to multiple factors, including long work hours, extensive political/bureaucratic policies and mandates paired with high individual teacher accountability, a relatively low salary, and diminished societal respect that can lead to bullying and harassment (Singer, 2019). Additional stressors include emotional exhaustion, depersonalization, a low sense of accomplishment, lack of resources, and lack of collegial support (Schonert-Reichl, 2017). These stressors have an impact on teachers' sense of agency, which is made worse when teachers are asked to implement policies that they disagree with or believe are unjust. The guilt, shame, and anger that follow from being put in this kind of position has been conceptualized as moral injury. One recent study examined the moral injury experienced by educators and argued that it was similar to that of military veterans, as teachers are often asked to uphold unfair policies and systems (Sugrue, 2020). These factors make it easy to see why the job can feel overwhelming and unsatisfying for these talented graduates.

Consider these adversarial conditions in terms of Bronfenbrenner's (1979) ecological model. Microsystems (immediate environments), mesosystems (connections between microsystems), exosystems (social and cultural structures), and macrosystems (institutional, economic, and legal systems) are all at play in toxic stress and mental health. Just as there is an interplay between risk and resiliency for children's mental health, the same is true for teachers.

Bronfenbrenner's (1979) ecological theory is concerned with human development, but it can serve as a helpful framework for thinking about how teachers can exercise their agency to make an impact on, interrupt, or influence each of Bronfenbrenner's systems. Indeed, Aguilar (2018) examines teacher resilience in the context of three domains similar to those of Bronfenbrenner's ecological model: individual resilience, organizational conditions, and systemic conditions. Aguilar states:

> Here is my theory of action: If we boost our resilience, then we will have more energy to address organizational and systemic conditions ... in acquiring the individual strategies, resilient educators can then transform their entire classroom as a subset of society, their school as a larger subset, and even the larger school district and system. Resilient educators may also have the energy to engage in conversation about the macro context and to take action to change it. To create the just and equitable society that I know so many of us yearn for, we need tremendous reserves of resilience.

We agree with Aguilar (2018) that teacher resilience or mental health is not simply an individual act or activity, although personal practices certainly can be helpful. We argue that developing competence, agency, and identity comes from engaging in as many aspects of Bronfenbrenner's systems as possible. We begin with a set of ideas centered around fostering resiliency in the exosystems and macrosystems in which teachers work. Then, we offer suggestions related to microsystems and mesosystems.

Building Resiliency within the Exosystem and Macrosystem

Although teachers can exercise their agency in the microsystems of their classrooms and schools, there also are opportunities to affect some of the larger systems that connect to their work. The exosystem consists of contexts that are not directly part of the microsystem of our work in schools but, nevertheless, have an impact on them. For example, a teacher's mother becomes ill and requires more care, thus drawing energy away from the teacher's work; or a partner loses a job, and a teacher has to take on additional responsibilities to try to make up for what was lost financially. The macrosystem consists of even broader cultural, legal, economic, and political systems that influence our lives. These systems afford teachers opportunities to engage as experts and advocates in ways that can be personally and professionally meaningful and sustaining. Below are a few ideas for how to develop community with others through organizational participation.

Build Community by Becoming Active in Professional Organizations

Although it is essential to find a home within a particular school, there are additional ways to be an active member of a profession. Leadership or service opportunities within a school district (e.g., textbook adoption committees or time as a teacher on special assignment to lead a particular initiative) are critical in feeling connected to the overall institution and the decisions made within it. One's labor union also can provide kinship and positive action with coworkers while making a difference. Knowing and being known by people in the larger professional community can lead to feeling more connected and valued. Being in the room as decisions are made allows teachers to exercise their voice and advocate on behalf of colleagues, students, and families. Even if the ultimate decision or policy is not to one's liking, understanding why it happened can be of some comfort.

International (e.g., International Reading Association), national (e.g., National Council of Teachers of Mathematics), or state professional organizations (e.g., California Association of Bilingual Teachers) can help teachers to find additional professional homes. Beyond building a sense of community through participation, these spaces can offer professional development opportunities, such as webinars and conferences, that allow teachers to renew their enthusiasm for their work as they learn. Some organizations also publish research journals and books aimed at practitioner audiences. The knowledge that comes from membership in these organizations can help teachers to build confidence in their expertise and their ability to make informed decisions, which can support them against adversity (Zee & Kooman, 2016).

A story from my (Amy's) career helps to show the power of what it can mean to invest in one's professional development in this way. While teaching fourth grade, I was confronted by my principal with a concern that my students were reading too much. This observation from my administrator came after she had noticed my students' reading for 30 minutes after lunch each day during "Drop Everything and Read" (DEAR) time. Although I loved seeing reluctant readers perusing the *Los Angeles Times* Sports page or overhearing two kids discussing their favorite comic book series due to this pedagogical practice, my principal disagreed. After receiving the feedback, I researched the value of independent reading time published by a professional literacy organization and found a study that helped me to make my case. After providing the article and my observations of the impact of independent reading on specific students, I was allowed to continue with the practice. (Note: this strategy also came in handy with parents who questioned my pedagogy—a stack of research that backs a teaching practice can go a long way in asserting one's professional authority.)

Avenues to work as an advocate for families, communities, children, and schools in the context of an organization that may hold some societal or political influence can be energizing as well. Many professional organizations publish position statements on pedagogical practices, offer suggestions on societal issues connected to education, and provide other types of leadership, such as political lobbying or formal testimony on policy and legislation that affects education locally and nationally. Although there may be ways for members to sit on committees that do this type of work, it is important to remember that teachers contribute to the common good by simply being members in good standing. Participation, whether through active service, reading the organization's formal recommendation, or signing a petition, also can expand notions of what is possible as teachers learn, grow, and advocate within a community.

A Sampling of Professional Organizations in Education

There are many local and state professional organizations dedicated to excellence in education. Check out district and state recommendations for local groups to join (the credential commission website is a great place to look). Below are a few national and international organizations that are considered reputable.

> American Association of School Librarians
> American Council on the Teaching of World Languages

American Library Association
American Speech-Language Hearing Association
Center for Applied Special Technology
Computer Using Educators (CUE)
Council for Exceptional Children
Getty Education
International Literacy Association
Literacy Research Association
National Art Education Association
National Arts and Education Network
National Association for Bilingual Education
National Association for the Education of Young Children
National Association for Gifted Children
National Council for Teachers of English
National Council for Teachers of Mathematics
National Parent Teacher Association
National Science Teachers Association
National Writing Project
TESOL International Organization

Reflection

- Are there professional organizations that you know of that you have considered joining? Which ones are they, and what about them appeals to you?
- What do you know about how these organizations provide opportunities for engagement and participation? What kinds of participation appeal to you? Where could you start?

Reading, Writing, and Storytelling as a Way to Understand and Advocate for Your Work

Another path toward building reserves of resiliency can include ongoing practices of reading, writing, and dialogue. Although this process can start by simply keeping a journal, it provides us with a means to access the power of social support by reflecting and then sharing our stories. Teacher book clubs or inquiry groups, connecting with colleagues and others via social media, and telling stories about life in the classroom to whomever will listen help teachers to reflect on classroom practices and better understand the importance of what they do. Reciprocally, others can then better connect with the needs of our schools and students and may even become allies in advocacy. By investing in our knowledge, we are better equipped to explore and propose solutions to some issues that may be draining our energy in the classroom.

Grassroots networking and partnerships can also be a powerful connector. One example of what this might look like comes from a friend who founded and directed a local independent preschool. Because funds were limited and the school had a deep commitment to teacher learning, the school's director reached out to other local preschools with similar values. Together, they formed a collective group that created common learning experiences for their faculties while sharing professional development costs. As teachers in these schools learned with and from one another through extended sessions with experts, observations of each other's schools, and travels together to learn from schools internationally, a grassroots network of outstanding professionals was created. Many members of this original group of teachers have now opened schools, taught classes at local community colleges, and founded nonprofit organizations that advocate for children and families and deepen commitments to teacher learning. In having a group of like-minded educators with a shared vision, this group's impact is being felt within and beyond their immediate school sites. Its teachers have been transformed by the work that they did and still do together.

When teachers invest in their knowledge through reading and writing, exercise their agency, and go public with their work with students, they demonstrate their potential as public intellectuals. By serving as examples and showing others what is possible, by engaging in professional organizations or creating their own grassroots networks of change, they garner respect for themselves and the profession. In this way, they are not only fighting for an educational system that is more socially, economically, politically, and environmentally just, but also working against the same phenomena that are contributing to the perils of burnout.

> **Reflection**
> - Do you spend time reflecting on your job, either alone or with others?
> - In what contexts do you share your thoughts? How is this helpful?
> - How might you expand this practice?

Creating Resiliency within the Microsystem and Mesosystem

What builds resilience will vary from person to person. In this section, we provide ideas on how to work against the challenges of emotional exhaustion, depersonalization, a limited sense of accomplishment, and lack of collegial support (Schonert-Reichl, 2017) within one's immediate microsystem (for this chapter, the individual classroom) and mesosystems (the school or school district). Because a critical theme of this book is the power of social ties to prevent problems and heal them when they occur, the ideas here will not center exclusively around what individuals can do for themselves but, instead, what individuals can do in relation to others.

Although out-of-school personal habits, such as healthy eating, sleeping, exercise, and time with friends and family, are important, the ideas below focus primarily on versions of self-care tied to the circumstances of the workday. As Neff and Germer (2018) note, because teachers serve as sources of care and support for students on an ongoing basis, self-care cannot just be something done outside school, like a workout at the gym. Instead, teachers must be present and grounded *as* they work.

Microsystem: Start with a Good Match

Schools can be found everywhere, and each campus has its own culture, often based on the school's leadership. That said, when looking for a professional home, you should cast a wide net to "find your people." The "right" place, the "right" team, and the "right" community are those that align with your values and gifts. Ahead of your search, clearly identify for yourself who you are as a teaching professional, including your core needs (which likely stem from your personal and professional values) and non-negotiable dealbreakers. Asking yourself, "What do I need?" in a job search is critical. Neff and Germer (2018) note that core values are housed in relationships, as they reflect how we engage with others. These ways of being in the world inform how we take care of and express ourselves. As Neff and Germer point out, we undermine our own potential for happiness when we are not living in alignment with our core values.

Because an individual's core needs should be foregrounded in a job search, once you discover a potential professional home, it is essential to tailor your cover letter and resume to demonstrate to the employer that you are the right fit for the position. Should you be granted an interview, ask questions to determine whether what the members of a school say they do is consistent with their values. Then look for evidence regarding whether this is the case. For example, you may read in a school's mission statement that the school values lifelong learning and then learn in an interview that the school does not offer a robust professional development program. When the mission and practice do not align, it is a signal that a particular school might not be working to its potential. Although you might decide that you are willing to join an imperfect institution because it is worth investing your time and energy for other reasons, it is also important to remember that you need only one job. Being picky about where that is can help to set you up for success.

Activity: How Do You Know Who You Are and What You Want?

Sometimes we spend so many years on a goal-setting treadmill that, when we are able to pursue a job, we are no longer sure who we are or what school context would be the right fit. Below is one way to figure out the answers.

Go on a "scavenger hunt" of your life to determine your understandings of yourself as an educator. Places to look for ideas include:

- Your lived experiences in the classroom so far. What did you appreciate as a student and want to preserve? What was frustrating to you that you feel must change? What kind of teacher do you envision yourself being for others?
- The essay you wrote to get into your teacher education program. What did you say about your motivation for entering the profession? What is now true after some time in the classroom?
- Any assignments you did during that program around creating a teaching philosophy, for example, showcasing your work with students. What are you proud of? Why? If you were to redo those assignments today, what would be preserved? What would be different?
- Any feedback that you received from faculty, mentor teachers, supervisors, or students. In other words, what do others say are your gifts and talents?
- Yourself. Look inward and pay close attention to yourself and your motivations for being a teacher: What draws you to this work? How do you know?

Once you have a picture of the kind of teacher you are, look to see how well your values, intentions, and skills match a particular school site. Is there enough of a match that you feel the position is a good fit? Is there room for you to grow professionally in this space? Does this school feel like "home" to you professionally? Look for a school with a mission statement that speaks to you, and then look for evidence on how its practices match its intentions.

Activity: How to Assess a School Setting

Most schools have a mission statement that describes their institutional values and practices. Before going to an interview, make sure to become aware of what a school says about what it is doing by reading the mission statement. Once you are on the campus, look for evidence that the mission is being carried out in various ways that include and go beyond pedagogy.

Mission statements might contain ideas about relationships, engagement, and desired outcomes. Below are some common phrases and examples of what you might look for as evidence that a school's practices are consistent with its mission.

Common phrases	Evidence
"Strong relationships"	Are students and teachers treating each other with respect? Do classroom behavior systems encourage intrinsic motivation in students? Is there evidence of socioemotional learning in the classroom? What do you notice about the relationships between adult professionals on the school campus? What do these professionals say about their relationships with families?
"Engaged learning"	Does the curriculum seem to resonate with students? Is it based on their interests, lived experiences, and communities? How is the work they do in school connected to real-life contexts? Is it culturally and linguistically sustaining? Do teachers also see themselves as learners?
"Lifelong learners"	How much student voice and agency do you notice in and out of the classroom? What is the role of reflection and vulnerability in the learning process? Are adult professionals on the school campus reflecting and learning as well?

Aguilar (2018) offers an extension of the theme of finding a professional home, reminding teachers that there are many roles to play in educating children and that we may not find our best role the first time. For example, when I (Amy) began my career, I took a high school Spanish teaching internship. This position seemed like an ideal fit, given how much I loved my secondary Spanish teachers when I was growing up and wanted to pay forward a love of the Spanish language. When the K–12 school that I was working at could not provide me with enough class periods of Spanish, I went to assist in the kindergarten for part of the day. Being open to new possibilities, I learned that I had a passion for language development, regardless of the age of the students. This led me to become a certificated elementary school teacher with a bilingual Spanish authorization and, eventually, a teacher education professor with specific expertise in language, literacy, and learning. Finding a professional niche can take time. Be patient, and don't be afraid to take on new opportunities just because they were not part of the original plan.

Microsystem: Create a Microsystem You Want to Be in Every Day

When you find the right fit in a school-home (or even if the fit isn't perfect), it is important to remember what you do have control over as a teacher: the classroom environment. The best part of being the adult in this scenario is that much of what happens, at least in setting the tone and expectations, is your decision. That begins with how you show up to work.

In the late fall, just when teacher candidates at our university are in a predictable cycle of intense stress, we ask them to conduct an audit of their self-care practices. The project, described below, is based on an activity developed by Jennings (2015), who discusses a human need for experiences and actions that represent the physical, emotional, intellectual, and spiritual domains of life. Physical activities include anything that helps your body, such as taking a nap or lifting weights. Emotional activities include what brings you joy, such as being with people you care about or being creative. Intellectual needs are fulfilled by opportunities to learn, such as when you are engaging in conversation or reading. Spiritual activities can include religious practices or any other existential act that helps you to locate and ground yourself in the universe (Jennings, 2015).

Teacher candidates spend a week logging their time on related activities in each area (physical, emotional, intellectual, and spiritual), within and outside of student teaching time. Many of these teachers recognize that these needs are met (or can be met) through their teaching and by activities outside of the classroom. They write in reflection papers that the exercise of documenting how they fill their proverbial buckets (and identify which domains need more focused attention) brings to consciousness a critical self-understanding. The exercise also informs them of how to concretely address an ethical need to show up to school as the most grounded, rested, present, and wise adult that they can be. They state that, when they do this exercise, it directly affects their ability to stay calm and patient with their students.

> **Engagement with the Four Domains of Life**
>
> Consider the domains discussed above and note what activities you do in each of the domains that build mental health and resilience. For each one, evaluate your engagement with that domain on the following scale: (1) I am not very engaged in this domain, (2) I have some engagement but perhaps not as much as I want, and (3) I am engaged in this domain in my life in ways that seem satisfying for now:
>
> - Physical
> - Emotional
> - Intellectual
> - Spiritual

Teachers' emotional awareness has been shown to have a meaningful impact on the classroom's social and academic climates. Schonert-Reichl (2017) notes that teachers who know how to facilitate caring relationships with and among their students often have classrooms in which student learning and socioemotional competency thrive. She explains that teachers who are more socially and culturally self-aware experience greater success in their work, which feeds their professional self-confidence and job satisfaction. For this reason, facilitating teacher knowledge around socioemotional learning and culturally responsive and sustaining instruction can be critical buffers against burnout.

Fortunately, teachers and students can develop their socioemotional skills simultaneously. Teachers can model techniques such as thinking aloud about their emotions, taking a deep breath and pausing when they are upset, naming and appreciating good moments and feelings, and practicing gratitude for their class and the experiences that they and their students are have having together. Teachers can then invite students to follow suit. Teachers and students can learn to practice traditional mindfulness techniques (such as focused breathing exercises), which can be found on apps. They can work together to create a prosocial environment through restorative practices and rituals, such as morning meetings and conflict resolution protocols in keeping with the ones mentioned in Chapter 6. In these ways, teachers can learn alongside their students, modeling coping mechanisms and ways of being in the world that contribute to having a healthy mind. In this way, they are creating a humane environment.

In addition to mindfulness practices in which teachers and students take time to cultivate presence and stillness, teachers can eliminate the use of multitasking during the school day (Note: Our brains do not multitask; they switch rapidly from one focus to another, which may not be the most efficient way to accomplish something). One way to do this is to pause after experiences of joyful learning and connection, which occur outside of mindfulness practice, to name and notice what just happened. Remembering and articulating that these are the moments that fulfill our purpose as teachers and learners is also valuable. Purposefully planning breaks in the day, as an individual or with your class, also can contribute to a culture of slowing down and appreciating ourselves and our work. It is also important to be present with and acknowledge experiences that feel negative. Finally, teachers should pay attention to the physical aesthetics of the classroom to create an atmosphere that is calming, relatively free of clutter, incorporates elements of the natural world, and reflects the people who work and learn in the space. Working in an environment that is beautiful and intentional is something that we all deserve.

> **Social Emotional Learning Skills**
>
> Above, we briefly discussed several strategies to promote positive mental health. Of the ones listed below, which do you now engage in and which would you like to incorporate into your daily practice with your students?
>
> - Thinking aloud about emotions
> - Taking a deep breath and pausing when upset
> - Naming and appreciating good moments and feelings
> - Practicing gratitude for the class and the experiences that you are having together
> - Traditional mindfulness
> - Restorative practices

Commit to a Habit of Self-compassion

Because many teachers enter the profession with the intent of helping others, making a difference in the world, or furthering social justice, a misstep in judgment can sometimes feel devastating. This feeling is often coupled with the lack of a full understanding of the impact of that mistake, creating a sense of insecurity. As educational psychologist Neff (2011) points out, a frame of self-compassion can help teachers to see that leaning into those moments of pain and learning how to comfort ourselves remind us of our humanity and connection to others and can have the potential to make us happier and more accepting human beings.

Self-compassion comprises three components: self-kindness, a sense of common humanity, and mindfulness (Neff & Germer, 2018). As discussed in Chapter 6, working in a helping

> - What commitment can I make in terms of time and resources to communicate moments of meaningful work and joyful learning to myself, my colleagues, my students, and their families? What might documentation do for me in terms of sustaining my own joy for what I do?

Conclusion

Teacher self-care, self-compassion, and self-renewal are necessities for a workforce that often needs to shoulder an overbearing responsibility for multiple societal issues. When teachers take care of themselves in the context of their work, there is an even greater potential for them to sustain themselves in a productive and meaningful career. The kind of joy, agency, and growth that comes from being in relationship with others as they teach has the potential to generate the momentum needed to take leadership roles outside of the classroom as well. In these ways, teachers can engage others to assist them in improving the experience of schooling for children, families, communities, and professionals themselves.

> **Reflection**
> - Which ideas in this chapter resonate with you? What additional avenues might you take in the name of self-care, self-compassion, and self-renewal in the teaching profession?
> - How do you see the intersection of the micro-, meso-, exo-, and macrosystems' playing out in your career as they relate to the potential for burnout? Which system(s) serve as the best means for you to address your energy as you work against this phenomenon?
> - How do you see the professional relationships that you have cultivated so far as connecting to prevention of burnout as a teacher? In what ways do they sustain you in your work?

Takeaways

- Build community by becoming active in professional organizations.
- Read, write, and tell stories to understand and advocate for your work.
- Develop a good match between you and your position.
- Create a microsystem that you want to be in every day.
- Commit to a habit of self-compassion.
- Find meaning in your work.
- See students as your partners.
- Reflect your work back to yourself, your students, and your community.

References

Aguilar, E. (2018). *Onward: Cultivating emotional resilience in educators*. Jossey Bass.

Ardell, A. L., & Curwen, M. S. (2021). "Multiple perspectives and many connections": Systems thinking and student voice. In L. Hogg, K. Stockbridge, C. Achieng-Evensen, & S. SooHoo (Eds.), *Pedagogies of with-ness: Students, teachers, voice and agency* (pp. 117–128). Meyers Education Press.

Bronfenbrenner, U. (1979). *The ecology of human development: Experiments by nature and design*. Harvard University Press.

Busby, E. (2019, February, 25). Teachers suffer more stress than other workers, study finds. *The Independent*. https://www.independent.co.uk/news/education/education-news/teachers-stress-professionals-mental-health-workload-national-foundation-educational-research-a8795691.html?fbclid=IwAR3qWVKbuA92FrP5sK2sK28yU5hPTTH9kRnUJ0qX4kPJPp35MQAWRVsMSNY

Davis, B., Sumara, D., & Luce-Kapler, R. (2015). *Engaging minds: Cultures of education and practices of teaching* (3rd ed.). Routledge.

Edwards, C., Gandini, L., & Forman, G. (1998). *The hundred languages of children: The Reggio Emilia approach—Advanced reflections* (2nd ed.). ABC-CLIO.

Ginwright, S. (2018, May 31). The future of healing: Shifting from trauma informed care to healing centered engagement. *Medium*. https://ginwright.medium.com/the-future-of-healing-shifting-from-trauma-informed-care-to-healing-centered-engagement-634f557ce69c

Harvard Project Zero & Reggio Children. (2001). *Making learning visible: Children as individual and group learners*. Reggio Children.

Ingersoll, R. M., Merrill, E., Stuckey, D., & Collins, G. (2018). Seven trends: The transformation of the teaching force—Updated October 2018. *CPRE Research Reports*. https://repository.upenn.edu/cpre_researchreports/108

Jennings, P. A. (2015). *Mindfulness for teachers: Simple skills for peace and productivity in the classroom*. W.W. Norton and Company.

Lips-Wiersma, M., & Morris, L. (2011). *The map of meaningful work: A practical guide to sustaining our humanity* (2nd ed.). Routledge.

Neff, K. (2011). *Self-compassion: The proven power of being kind to yourself*. Harper Collins.

Neff, K., & Germer, C. (2018). *The mindful self-compassion workbook: A proven way to accept yourself, build inner strength, and thrive*. Guilford Press.

Schonert-Reichl, K. A. (2017). Social and emotional learning and teachers. *The Future of Children, 27*(1), 137–155.

Singer, S. (2019). Gadfly on the wall blog: Teachers are more stressed out than you probably think. *National Educational Policy Center, University of Colorado Boulder*. https://nepc.colorado.edu/blog/teachers-stressed

Sugrue, E. P. (2020). Moral injury among professionals in in K–12 education. *American Education Research Journal, 57*(1), 43–68. https://doi.org/10.3102/0002831219848690

Zee, M., & Kooman, H. M. Y. (2016). Teacher self-efficacy and its effects on classroom processes, student academic adjustment, and teacher well-being: A synthesis of 40 years of research. *Review of Educational Research, 86*(4), 981–1015.

Appendix

Questions as a Guide to the Recognition of Mental Health Problems

1. What, specifically, is the student doing or not doing that troubles you?
2. How have these behaviors impacted the student's learning? How do you think these behaviors affect the student socially?
3. Do these behaviors seem typical or atypical?
    a. Are these behaviors developmentally appropriate?
    b. What would the consequences of these behaviors be later in the child's development?
    c. How intense are these problems?
        i. How long?
        ii. How frequent?
        iii. Rate on a scale of 1–10
4. What do you think the student is feeling? What do you think the student is thinking about your class, school, and his or her life in general?
5. What is going on in a student's life that might contribute to these behaviors?
6. Who is this student connected to in a supportive way?

Printed in the United States
by Baker & Taylor Publisher Services